BRITISH RAILWAYS BOARD

The Reshaping of British Railways

PART 1: REPORT

The Reshaping of British Railways

REPORT AND MAPS

LONDON: HER MAJESTY'S STATIONERY OFFICE

ORIGINAL FACSIMILE

BRITISH RAILWAYS BOARD

The Reshaping of British Railways

PART I: REPORT

LONDON:

HER MAJESTY'S STATIONERY OFFICE

1963

The Reshaping of British Railways

i

The Reshaping of British Railways

FOREWORD

The formulation of plans for the reshaping of British Railways has been foreshadowed by numerous references in Parliament, and in other places, ever since the Prime Minister, speaking in the House on 10th March, 1960, said:—

> 'First the industry must be of a size and pattern suited to modern conditions and prospects. In particular, the railway system must be remodelled to meet current needs, and the modernisation plan must be adapted to this new shape.'

It may appear that the lapse of three years between the date when the original reference was made to the necessity for reshaping the railways and the emergence of a plan is excessive, but there are two reasons why it took so long.

In the first place, attention was devoted to the reorganisation of the British Transport Commission structure. As a result, it was not until the latter part of 1961, after the first steps had been taken to give effect to the structural reorganisation described in the White Paper on Reorganisation of the Nationalised Transport Undertaking (Cmnd. 1248), that positive steps were taken towards planning the future shape of the railways.

Secondly, there had never before been any systematic assembly of a basis of information upon which planning could be founded, and without which the proper role of the railways in the transport system as a whole could not be determined. The collection of this information was itself a massive task and it is, perhaps, more surprising that it was brought to a useful stage in just over a year than that it should have taken so long.

Throughout these investigations and the preparation of this report the British Railways Board has had it in mind that its duty is to employ the assets vested in it, and develop or modify them, to the best advantage of the nation. Also, because the ultimate choice of what is considered most advantageous must be made by the nation, it is a basic responsibility of the Board to provide, as objectively and comprehensively as possible, information which makes clear the range and nature of the choice.

In general, people will wish to base a choice between alternative modes of transport upon consideration of quality of service and the cost of obtaining it. It must be recognised, however, that, in the transport field more than in many others, the judgment of some quality factors is largely subjective, that individual convenience and total social benefit are not necessarily compatible, and that competing forms of transport cannot be costed on strictly comparable bases. For these reasons, none of the major proposals for reshaping the railway system which are made in this report is based upon attempted close judgments between ratios of quality to cost for competing systems of transport. Proposals have,

1

on the other hand, been influenced by major differences in the more measurable aspects of service quality, such as speed and reliability. They have also been influenced by major disparities in cost arising from the inherent characteristics of the various forms of transport, and by major disparities between the value of the service provided, measured in terms of what people are prepared to pay for it, and the cost of providing it.

It is, of course, the responsibility of the British Railways Board so to shape and operate the railways as to make them pay, but, if it is not already apparent from the preceding paragraphs, it must be clearly stated that the proposals now made are not directed towards achieving that result by the simple and unsatisfactory method of rejecting all those parts of the system which do not pay already or which cannot be made to pay easily. On the contrary, the changes proposed are intended to shape the railways to meet present day requirements by enabling them to provide as much of the total transport of the country as they can provide well. To this end, proposals are directed towards developing to the full those parts of the system and those services which can be made to meet traffic requirements more efficiently and satisfactorily than any available alternative form of transport, and towards eliminating only those services which, by their very nature, railways are ill-suited to provide.

The point at issue here is so important that it is worthwhile to emphasise it by expressing the underlying thought in a different way.

The profitability or otherwise of a railway system is dependent on a number of external influences which may change markedly from time to time, important among them being decisions affecting the freedom of use, cost of use, and availability of roads. For this and other reasons, it is impossible to plan the maximum use of railways consistent with profitability, for years ahead, without some risk that it will prove, in the event, that services have been over-provided and that overall profitability is not achieved. On the other hand, to retain only those parts of the existing system which are virtually certain to be self-supporting under any reasonably probable future conditions would lead to grave risk of destroying assets which, in the event, might have proved to be valuable.

Confronted with this dilemma, arising from the impossibility of assessing future conditions and future profitability very reliably, the Railways Board have put forward proposals for reshaping the system which are conservative with regard to closures and restrainedly speculative with regard to new developments, but which are all directed towards shaping the system to provide rail transport for only that part of the total national traffic pattern which costing and commonsense consideration show to have characteristics favourable to rail transport.

The plan is not carried to the stage where it purports to answer the question, 'How much of the railway can ultimately be made to pay?'. This answer will emerge only after experience has shown how much benefit springs from elimination of those parts of the system which are obviously unsound, and the extent to which the good parts of the railways' system and traffic can be improved by: cost savings, better quality of service, better operating methods, and attraction of favourable traffic. Nevertheless, the firm proposals included in the plan are expected to lead to substantial improvements in the financial position. Perhaps even more important, they set a clear course for the railways, in a general direction which must be right and which can be followed with vigour without any danger of eliminating too much or of incurring grossly wasteful expenditure before the position can be reviewed.

The changes proposed, and their phasing, are certainly not too drastic if regarded as a means of correcting the present departure of the railways from their proper role in the transport system as a whole. It is recognised, however, that changes of the magnitude of those proposed will inevitably give rise to many difficulties affecting railway staff, the travelling public, and industry. The Railways Board will do all that it can to ameliorate these difficulties, consistent with its responsibility for making railways an efficient and economic component in the transport system, but the Board knows that it will not be able to solve all problems unaided.

THE NATURE OF THE PROBLEM

The railways emerged from the war at a fairly high level of activity, but in a poor physical state. They were able to pay their way, because road transport facilities were still limited, and they continued to do so until 1952. From then onwards, however, the surplus on operating account declined progressively. After 1953 it became too small to meet capital charges, after 1955 it disappeared, and by 1960 the annual loss on operating account had risen to £67·7 m. This rose further to £86·9 m. in 1961.

In 1955, a modernisation plan was embarked upon. It was a plan to modernise equipment, but it did not envisage any basic changes in the scope of railway services or in the general mode of operation of the railway system. It was expected that the substitution of electric and diesel haulage for steam, concentration of marshalling yards, reduction in number and increased mechanisation of goods depots, re-signalling, and the introduction of other modern equipment, would make the railways pay by reducing costs and attracting more traffic.

By 1960, however, it had become apparent that the effects of modernisation were neither so rapid nor so pronounced as had been forecast, that the downward trend in some railway traffics would persist, and the operating losses were likely to go on increasing unless radical changes were made.

There is a considerable scope for cost reduction by a multiplicity of economies over the whole field of railway operations, and vigorous efforts are being made to achieve them. Nevertheless, it was obvious, even before detailed investigation started, that neither modernisation nor more economical working could make the railways viable in their existing form, and that a reshaping of the whole pattern of the business would be necessary as well.

Ever since major amalgamations started, the business of the railways has been, from a financial point of view, a mixture of good, bad, and indifferent routes, services and traffics. Nevertheless, the circumstances which obtained throughout the major period of railway history in Britain—conditions of near monopoly, obligation to carry, and statutory fixing of rates without relationship to costs—all tended to cause accountancy to be limited to global accounts for each of the independent railway companies. As the companies merged, the accounting units became larger without an offsetting increase in detail, and this continued to be the position when all the railways were combined by nationalisation.

3

While these conditions existed, and while the railways were able to make a profit on their business as a whole, the unknown degree of cross-subsidisation involved in carrying bad traffic on the back of financially good traffic was very largely ignored. Now, however, after the post-war growth of competition from road transport, it is no longer socially necessary for the railways to cover such a preponderant part of the total variety of internal transport services as they did in the past, and it is certainly not possible for them to operate profitably if they do so.

Road competition has forced down rates on good railway traffics to the point where they are quite incapable of subsidising the very costly provision of services to handle poor rail traffics. Even worse, the burdening of good traffics with costs arising from bad ones has led to the transfer to road of a considerable volume of traffic which railways are better able to handle, in order to preserve on rail traffics which could be handled better by road.

It is this situation which necessitates a much more analytical examination of the Railways' business with a view to reshaping their system, their mode of operation, and their pattern of services and traffics.

ANALYSIS OF THE PROBLEM

The logical approach to the problem of shaping, or reshaping a railway system is:—

   (i) to determine the basic characteristics which distinguish railways as a mode of transport;
   (ii) to determine under what conditions these characteristics enable railways to be the best available form of transport;
   (iii) to determine to which parts of the total national pattern of transport requirements these conditions apply;
   (iv) to shape the railway route system and services so as to take advantage of favourable circumstances wherever they exist.

Unfortunately, simple as this sequence appears, there is no single or simple way of accumulating and presenting information which enables it to be followed in quantitative terms. It is, nevertheless, a very useful beginning to consider, even in general terms, what are the basic characteristics of railways and under what circumstances these characteristics are likely to make railways the best available form of transport.

Railways are distinguished by the provision and maintenance of a specialised route system for their own exclusive use. This gives rise to high fixed costs. On the other hand, the benefits which can be derived from possession of this high cost route system are very great.

Firstly, it permits the running of high capacity trains, which themselves have very low movement costs per unit carried. Secondly, it permits dense flows of traffic and, provided the flows are dense, the fixed costs per unit moved are also low. Thirdly, it permits safe, reliable, scheduled movements at high speed.

In a national system of transport we should, therefore, expect to find railways concentrating upon those parts of the traffic pattern which enable them to derive sufficient benefit from these three advantages to offset their unavoidable burden of high system cost. In other words, we should expect the provision of railways to be limited to routes over which it is possible to develop dense flows of traffic, of the kinds which lend themselves to movement in trainload quantities and which, in part at least, benefit from the speed and reliability which the railways are capable of achieving. Moreover, we should expect that, having been concentrated upon traffics matched to the advantageous features of rail transport, the system would then be operated so as to develop those features to the full.

In all that follows, we shall seek to show, as quantitatively as possible, how far the system departs from this condition at present, and to decide what changes are necessary to put matters right. To this end, a first step is a detailed examination of the existing rail system, its pattern of traffic, and its mode of operation.

EXAMINATION OF THE PRESENT STATE OF THE RAILWAYS

The most obvious ways of subdividing the railway business as a whole, for the purpose of detailed examination, are in relation to:

(a) units and sub-units of general managerial responsibility;
(b) functional subdivision;
(c) types of traffic;
(d) parts of the physical system.

No one of these modes of subdivision is, alone, sufficient to lead to understanding of such a large and complex business as that of British Railways, nor can any one of them be pursued in a manner which is completely accurate and reliable. For those reasons, some use has been made of all of them, so as to create a more detailed and reliable picture by the combination of several modes of study.

Subdivisions along the lines of (a) and (b) fall within the scope of normal accountancy. As has already been mentioned, however, railway accountancy has been limited, very largely, to global accounts for the railways as a whole. In consequence, very little information of the kind which could be derived by a thoroughgoing breakdown along the lines (a) and (b) was available. Moreover, because an accountancy system cannot be modified and extended so as to produce much more detailed results quickly, in an organisation of the size of the railways, the main attack on the problem was by subdivision along lines (c) and (d). To build the picture, however, it is convenient to start with the British Railways' accounts.

The figures presented are those for 1961 and, with minor exceptions, cost figures used throughout the Report relate to that year. The reason is that this was the latest year for which fully detailed cost data could be made available during the course of the investigation, and it was also the year in which the special traffic studies were made.

In a situation as changeable as that of the railways, no year can be described as typical. The year 1961 was not a good one from the traffic point of view, because the recession in the steel industry affected the latter part of it. In this respect, therefore, it was worse than 1960, but it was better than 1962, and it is not yet known whether 1963 will be better or worse. Also, although substantial economies were made in 1962, there were two increases in wage rates during that year which amounted to just over 9 per cent. and the working week was reduced.

It is known that the conclusions reached would all have been substantially the same had they been based upon figures for 1960, and there is no reason to think that they would be different were it possible to use figures for 1962 or the early part of 1963. Therefore, the Railways Board is satisfied that although the figures used throughout the Report are not, and could not be, completely up-to-date, they form a sound basis for decision making.

5

Consolidated Revenue Account

Gross Receipts:		£m.	£m.
Passenger		157·5	
Freight (including parcels and mails)		306·7	
Miscellaneous		10·5	
		———	474·7
Working Expenses:			
Train and vehicle operating expenses		187·5	
Maintenance of rolling stock		122·2	
Other traffic expenses		92·7	
Signalling expenses		39·1	
Maintenance of way and structures		85·4	
General		22·6	
Collection and delivery by road		22·1	
		571·6	
Deduct internal charges raised for transport charges		10·0	
		———	561·6
Net receipts			86·9
			(*Deficit*)

Interest and other central charges amounted to £49 m., making a total deficit of £135·9 m. Additionally, a sum of £23·4 m. was charged to Special Account (pursuant to Section 3 of the Transport (Railway Finances) Act, 1957) in respect of interest for the year on borrowings during the years 1958 to 1961 for capital purposes.

Functional Split of Expenses

This table shows a re-allocation of the Working Expenses of £561·6 m. according to operational functions:—

Train Working:—		£m.	£m.
Locomotives	Provision, maintenance, stabling and servicing	55·9	
Carrying units	Provision, maintenance, stabling and servicing:—		
Multiple units, carriages and parcels vans		55·0	
Wagons		46·1	
Operating wages		39·8	
Fuel, water and lubricants		52·3	
		———	249·1
Marshalling			20·3
Shunting			29·4
Terminal handling and facilities			64·9
Documentation			26·0
Collection and delivery by road			22·1
Miscellaneous (including publicity and claims) ..			6·9
Track and signalling			110·5
General administration			32·4
TOTAL EXPENSES			561·6

6

This re-allocation to operational functions of the Working Expenses as shown in the Accounts is the first stage in the production of the analysis referred to in the following section.

ANALYSIS BY TYPES OF TRAFFIC

With the growth of the Traffic Costing Service, figures on the lines of the table which follows have been prepared annually, showing the breakdown of revenue and costs between the main classes of traffic for British Railways as a whole. To do this, it is necessary to allocate many costs which are not identifiably associated with particular traffics. Such allocations cannot be made in a manner which is beyond dispute, but by dealing with cost elements individually and allocating them in the manner which seems most appropriate for each, results can be produced which provide a sound basis for general conclusions. The figures are shown in Table No. 1.

It will be seen that, in 1961, none of the main classes of traffic covered their full costs, with the exception of coal, which yielded a small margin of net revenue. Therefore, none of the traffic groups can be considered good, in an absolute sense, but there is a wide spread in their relative merit which reflects the extent to which they permit movement by dense flows of well loaded trains.

Thus, in the passenger field, stopping-trains are by far the worst loss maker. These trains, which derive little advantage from the speed of rail movement, are known to be very lightly loaded and to run, very largely, on routes which carry little traffic of any kind. Against direct cost alone they show losses almost equal to total receipts, and the overall loss is nearly twice receipts. On the other hand, fast and semi-fast services, provided by through trains which mostly load well and operate over the routes with high traffic levels, show a substantial margin of receipts over direct costs, even though the group as a whole falls short of paying its full share of system cost.

In the freight field the disparity between classes of traffic is just as great. Wagon-load general merchandise, which loads badly and gives rise to very little through train movement is a bad loss maker. Sundries traffic is bad for the same reason. The two freight traffics which show the best margin over direct cost are minerals and coal. Of these, coal gives a small margin of profit over full cost, while mineral traffic falls just short of doing so. These are classes of freight which give rise to a much higher proportion of through movement of well loaded trains than the others.

The allocations of traffics to groups is necessarily somewhat arbitrary and the traffics within any one group are far from homogeneous. Within groups of traffic which are relatively good as a whole there may well be some bad loss makers, and in groups which are bad, there may be some good streams of traffic. Therefore, although these figures for main traffic groups are informative in a broad sense, they fall far short of providing a basis for selective reshaping of the railways' traffic pattern. Also, because they give no information about the way in which traffic varies in mixture and density over the route system, they give no clear guidance as to how the physical system should be changed. For that purpose, a more detailed analysis is necessary.

Before more detailed consideration of particular types of traffic, however, it is necessary to say something about the route system itself and the distribution of traffic over it.

7

REVENUE AND ASSESSED COSTS BY MAIN TRAFFICS FOR BRITISH RAILWAYS, 1961

Table No. 1

Type of traffic	Receipts	Direct costs	Margin—surplus or *shortfall* of receipts over direct costs	Allocated indirect cost	Net revenue or *deficit* over total cost	Train miles	
	£m.	£m.	£m.	£m.	£m.	m.	
Passenger							
Fast and semi-fast	91·2	72·7	18·5	40·3	*21·8*	80·0	
Stopping	30·8	56·9	*26·1*	29·9	*55·9*	91·4	
Suburban	39·8	40·3	·5	24·5	*25·0*	58·2	
Total	161·8	169·9	*8·1*	94·6	*102·7*	229·6	
Freight by coaching train, mainly parcels and mails.	57·3	40·2	17·1	10·3	6·8		
						Wagon miles	*Tons*
						m.	m.
Freight							
Coal	108·3	83·5	24·8	22·0	2·8	913	145·7
Minerals	44·5	36·9	7·6	11·3	3·7	459	54·3
General Merchandise:							
Wagon-load	64·8	96·6	*31·8*	22·0	*53·8*	1,139	34·4
Sundries	38·0	51·5	*13·5*	7·8	*21·3*	462	3·8
Total	255·6	268·5	12·9	63·1	*76·0*	2,973	238·2
GRAND TOTAL	474·7	478·6	3·9	168·0	*171·9*		

The estimated costs in this table include interest and the provision for depreciation is calculated in terms of present money values.

BRITISH RAILWAYS' ROUTE SYSTEM AND THE DISTRIBUTION OF TRAFFIC DENSITY

In 1961, British Railways had a total route mileage of 17,830 and a running track mileage of 34,150.

The route mileage was made up approximately as follows:—

No. of tracks	Route miles	Miles open for freight only
Route with four tracks or over ..	1,500	100
Route with three tracks	400	100
Route with double track	10,000	1,200
Single track	5,900	2,700
	17,800	4,100

The total cost of maintaining this route system and of maintaining and operating the associated signalling system, exclusive of any allocation of interest on the capital employed, is £110 m. per annum. This is the cost of providing only the route on which trains can be run, i.e. the cost of providing the signalled track.

The estimated costs per route mile and the total costs of track in the various maintenance categories are shown below. Estimates in this form can only be broad approximations, but they serve to show the high cost of even low category routes.

Maintenance category	No. of tracks	Route miles	Estimated annual costs	
			Per mile £	Total £m.
A	Triple and over	1,100	15,000	16·5
	Double	3,000	8,250	24·7
B	Triple and over	800	11,000	8·8
	Double	3,500	7,250	25·4
	Single	300	4,000	1·2
C	Double	2,500	6,250	15·6
	Single	2,100	3,500	7·3
D	Double	1,000	3,500	3·5
	Single	3,500	2,000	7·0
		17,800		£110·0m.

The total cost of providing the route system, which, it should be emphasised, excludes the costs of associated sidings, yards, stations, and depots, amounts to nearly a quarter of the railways' total revenue. This is a fixed cost, in the full sense of the term, all the while the route system remains unchanged, and its high level emphasises the necessity for matching the railway system to available traffics so as to ensure a high average level of loading. Moreover, the figures for the cost per mile of various categories of route make it clear that quite high traffic densities are necessary, even on single track route, to cover route cost alone.

9

The capital cost of providing sidings, yards, stations and depots is just as firmly fixed as the cost of providing route, but the cost of operating these facilities does vary to some extent with the level of traffic using them. Even so, the extent of this variation is small, especially on a short term basis, and a large part of shunting and terminal costs must be regarded as fixed, all the while the associated route system remains unchanged, or until stations are actually closed, or closed to some forms of traffic.

It is these considerations which make so interesting the information derived from the traffic density surveys, the results of which are presented more fully in Appendix 1. In what immediately follows, reference is made only to salient features, but further references are made in subsequent sections, where we return to considerations of various classes of traffic.

The traffic surveys, which were made in great detail, extended over only one week, the week ending on 23rd April, 1961, because it was impossible to continue the massive recording effort involved for a longer period. It was realised, therefore, that conclusions about some streams of traffic and about some parts of the system which are affected by seasonal changes could not be based firmly on the traffic surveys alone. Subject to this limitation, however, there can be little doubt about the general reliability of the picture revealed.

The tables and graphs in Appendix 1 show how pronounced is the disparity in loading between heavily loaded and lightly loaded parts of the route system.

One third of the route mileage carries only 1 per cent. of the total passenger miles. Similarly, one third of the mileage carries only 1 per cent. of the freight ton miles of British Railways. The lightly used part of the system includes most of the single track branch line, of which there are 5,900 miles and of which 2,700 miles are open to freight traffic only. The proportion of British Railways' total passenger and freight revenue corresponding with this proportion of total traffic movement is £4½ m., while the cost of providing this route is some £20 m.

One half of the total route mileage carries about 4 per cent. of the total passenger miles. Similarly, one half of the mileage carries about 5 per cent. of the total freight ton miles of British Railways. The corresponding apportionment of total passenger and freight revenue is £20 m., and the estimated cost of providing this part of the track is of the order of £40 m. Therefore, in so far as it is reasonable to judge earnings in terms of the traffic movement provided, one half of the system earns far less than sufficient to cover the cost of providing route to permit the movement, with no allowance whatever for movement or other costs. By contrast, the other half of the system has earnings which cover its route costs more than six times.

It is recognised that the foregoing basis of consideration does not take account of the actual nature of the traffics on lightly loaded lines, of any special cost and charging feature associated with these traffics, nor of any contributory value which they may have to the remainder of the system. These matters will be considered later, however, and it will be found that so far from being exceptionally good traffics, most of the traffics fed to the rest of the system are of the less favourable kinds, and that their contribution of marginal revenue is small if not negative.

The disparities in the flow of traffics through stations are even more pronounced than those found in relation to routes. This is not surprising, because apart from the large variation in the size of the stations themselves, many of the smaller ones are on routes which are also lightly loaded.

In April 1961, British Railways had about 7,000 stations open to traffic, equivalent to one for every 2½ miles of route, and the distribution of stations over the route system with indications of their passenger and freight traffic levels are shown in Maps Nos. 3 and 4.

An analysis of the passenger receipts arising at passenger stations, excluding some very little used ones and unstaffed halts, was made from very complete records kept in 1960. As will be seen from Table No. 4 and Figure No. 2 in Appendix 1, one third of the stations produced less than 1 per cent. of the total passenger receipts and one half of the stations produced only 2 per cent. At the other end of the scale 34 stations, or less than 1 per cent. of the total, produced 26 per cent. of the receipts.

Of the freight stations, one third produced less than 1 per cent. of the station freight receipts and one half of the stations produced less than 3 per cent.

The total revenue derived from the least used half of the total number of stations and the cost of running them is set out below.

£m. per annum

Receipts from:

Originating passenger, parcels and other coaching train traffics at the least used 50 per cent. of all passenger stations	4·8
Freight traffic forwarded from the least used 50 per cent. of all freight stations	1·7
Estimated cost of least used 50 per cent. of all stations ..	9·0

From these figures, which are not highly accurate, but which are approximately correct, it will be seen that the gross revenue derived from traffic of all kinds flowing from the least used half of the total number of British Railways' stations does not match the cost of the stations themselves. In other words, it makes no contribution whatever to route costs, to movement costs, nor to terminal costs at the other end of its transit. There can be no question, therefore, that the railways would be better off financially if a high proportion of the stations were closed, even if this resulted in a total loss of the traffic passing through them.

MORE DETAILED CONSIDERATION
OF THE MAIN GROUPS OF TRAFFIC

The foregoing general considerations focus attention upon the extreme unprofitability of some broad classes of traffic, as they are handled at present, and also upon the highly questionable value of much of the lightly loaded route mileage and of many of the small stations. Nevertheless, before firm conclusions can safely be drawn as to the desirability of closing particular routes, or of deliberately rejecting particular types of traffic, it is necessary to examine the mixture of traffics in each broad class in more detail, and to determine what

11

parts of the total traffic mixture are associated with particular routes. It is also necessary to consider the potential effects of improved handling of traffic and the possibilities of attracting more or better traffics.

The extent to which this has been found possible is described in sections which follow.

PASSENGER SERVICES

The distribution of passenger traffic over the routes of British Railways is shown by Map No. 1. Numerous references will be made to this map in following sections, where passenger traffics are considered in the three main groups which have already been referred to, namely:—

Fast and semi-fast train services.

Stopping-train services.

Suburban services.

The characteristics which distinguish these three types of service are clear, even though the groups merge into each other so that sharp boundaries between them can only be drawn arbitrarily.

Fast and Semi-Fast Trains

Fast and semi-fast trains provide inter-city services. They depend, for the attraction of traffic, upon the provision of rapid transits between the centres of population which they serve and upon well-chosen departure and arrival times in relation to the social and business habits of the community. To achieve the speed required they must be limited-stop trains, and to be successful financially they must draw a substantial number of passengers from the cities which they link. In general, the greater the distances covered by such services the more closely the number and timing of trains can be matched to the volume of demand, so that train loadings can be kept high. Also, because such services normally operate over densely loaded routes where the system cost is well covered by the total traffic, there is less reason to run lightly loaded trains which yield very little margin over their own direct costs, since they may displace more profitable traffic.

With a few minor exceptions, fast and semi-fast services are located upon only those routes shown as full lines on the traffic density map (Map No. 1), and on those lines, away from the urban areas, they carry a high proportion of the total passenger flow.

To date, receipts from fast and semi-fast inter-city trains have been fairly stable and may be expected to remain so. They have not, however, kept pace with rising costs and the margin of receipts over direct costs does not make the contribution to the system which it should.

Inter-city distances in Britain are such that the squeezing out of rail traffic by the combined assault of air over the longer distances and the private car over the shorter distances is far less serious here than in larger and less densely populated countries such as the United States, where the process is almost complete.

Even though main road congestion is being reduced in many places, urban congestion remains at such a level as to discourage use of private cars for even medium distance journeys between large centres of population on grounds of

12

speed and comfort, and on cost for the individual traveller. On longer journeys, the adverse effect of terminal congestion is relatively less important, but the wear and tear of a long road journey then becomes an important deterrent. Therefore, for most of those passengers who make up the steady, year round, component of long distance travel, i.e. people travelling on business who rate their convenience and comfort highly, rail will remain preferable to road transport, provided that continuing attention is given to the speed, reliability and comfort of trains.

Air transport is not competitive in terms of speed for inter-city distances of less than about 200 miles, nor is it competitive in terms of cost except while operating as the minority carrier able to keep a high load factor by creaming from the total flow. This restricts the routes over which air competes seriously with rail to the London–Manchester, London–Newcastle and London–Scotland routes.

On the Scottish routes, air makes quite serious inroads into the loading of day trains, and will continue to do so. Even though trains may be speeded up, they will not match city-to-city transit times by air over such a distance, and erosion of daytime rail traffics between London and Scotland will probably continue to the point where some trains will have to be withdrawn. On the other hand, sleeper trains between London and Scotland continue to attract a satisfactory level of traffic, and there is good reason to suppose that they can be improved and increased.

On the Manchester route, rail and air are more nearly matched on time, and the difference will be reduced to a negligible level when rail times are reduced to $2\frac{3}{4}$ hours, as they will be with the completion of electrification of the route. Comfort will then become a predominant factor in rail/air competition, with the balance of advantage potentially in favour of rail for the journey as a whole.

For the reasons outlined, the general level of traffic on fast and semi-fast trains is expected to hold up well. As a group, these services make a substantial contribution to system cost, and their profitability can certainly be improved by detailed attention to individual services and trains. There is, therefore, no doubt about the continuation of the railways' inter-city passenger services on substantially the present broad pattern, so long as the main line network remains in being, adequately supported by other traffics. For this reason, it was thought unnecessary to include a rapid detailed examination of all the fast train services among the special studies connected with reshaping of the railways.

This does not mean that British Railways feel complacent about their inter-city services, nor that services will not be studied with a view to improving them. Improvements have and are being made, and will continue.

Some patterns for the future have already been set. The introduction of the Blue Pullman services between London and Birmingham, London and Manchester, and London and Swansea, with journey times of 1 hr. 55 min., 3 hrs. 10 min., and 3 hrs. 35 min. respectively, heralded the luxury train of the future.

The diesel-worked hourly day service between King's Cross and Newcastle, including trains in each direction which cover the $268\frac{1}{2}$ miles in four hours, compares favourably with the oft-quoted pre-war service in both frequency and capacity.

Where a demand capable of supporting quality services covered by supplementary charges is seen to exist, they will be introduced.

13

Competitive railway building in the past led not only to duplication of main arteries between some of the principal cities, but also to duplication of passenger stations and all the ancillary facilities such as carriage and cleaning sidings, motive power depots, buildings and equipment, which go with large terminals. Very little has been done, so far, to rationalise the main line passenger services which use alternative routes and terminals, but it is clear, in many cases, that concentration on selected routes and stations would provide equal or better services and permit substantial economies.

For example, studies of the possibilities at Leeds and Bradford, each of which has two large stations, are in an advanced stage. The need to retain separate main line services to Exeter and the West via both the Southern and Western routes is being examined. The Caledonian, the Glasgow and South Western, and the North British Companies left a legacy of four large terminals in Glasgow. The London and North Western and Midland Companies provided duplicate routes into Carlisle. Birmingham is served today by two Regions' services from London. The future of all these, and other comparable parallel routes and duplicate facilities, is being determined, and in some cases discussions are already taking place with civic authorities who are most anxious to collaborate in the development of sites which will be released by concentration schemes.

Before leaving the subject of fast and semi-fast services, it is necessary to comment upon seasonal variations. What has been said so far relates to the steady inter-city traffics, not to the summer holiday and public holiday peaks.

This peak traffic differs from the steady traffic in two important respects :—

    (a) much of it is far less profitable than the steady traffic, and

    (b) it is being eroded much more by the growth of private transport.

Total passenger traffic during the months of June to September, in 1961, exceeded the average for the remaining eight months of the year by 18 per cent. in June, 47 per cent. in July, 43 per cent. in August, and 21 per cent. in September. Ten years earlier, corresponding figures were 48 per cent. in June, 96 per cent. in July, 87 per cent. in August and 44 per cent. in September, which shows how the summer peak has diminished, in spite of developments of holidays with pay, greater general affluence, and overwhelming evidence of greater holiday travel. There can be no doubt that the decline in the rail peak is almost entirely due to the growth of family motoring, and the trend is likely to continue. There has been a similar decline in the public holiday weekend peaks, for the same reason, but these peaks remain very sharp.

Although the figures quoted relate to British Railways passenger traffic as a whole, a predominant part of the total additional traffic in holiday periods falls upon fast and semi-fast train services and the actual peak on some trains, particularly at weekends, may be very many times the normal level of loading.

In so far as the increased traffic arising in a peak period can be carried by the regular time-tabled trains, the yield from it is almost all net revenue. Up to that level it is very welcome financially, but the situation changes as soon as the traffic rises to a level necessitating extra trains. Moreover, because the capacity of many fast train services is well matched to the steady traffic, they are not able to absorb very large additional loads unless extra trains are put on.

Extra trains are very expensive to run, and may easily cause a loss which more than offsets any gain from increased traffic on the regular trains, especially if the extras are themselves only part filled and if there is no balancing return working for engines, vehicles and men. Such trains give rise to a high proportion of overtime working and they depend upon the availability of reserve coaching stock which is expensive to supply, maintain, and assemble, and which is idle for most of the year. The extent to which reserve stock has been held to cover peak demands in the past, and its gross under-utilisation, is shown by the following table, which relates to 1959:—

Total number of gangwayed coaches allocated to fast and semi-fast services	18,500
Number in year-round service	5,500
Additional vehicles for regular summer service	2,000
Available for high peak service	8,900
Under repair	2,100

A large number of the coaches available for high peak traffic were only required on a limited number of occasions as the following table, relating to the last 6,000 vehicles in the fleet, shows:—

Number of Coaches	Required on not more than:
2,000	10 occasions
2,000	14 occasions
2,000	18 occasions

The annual cost of providing the 6,000 coaches was £3·4m. Against this it was estimated that they only earned £0·5m. after allowing for all other costs of the movements concerned.

Since the beginning of 1959 the number of passenger-carrying gangway coaches has been reduced by 5,584 and by the end of 1965 stock will not be available for use at high peak periods. Efforts will be made to control these peaks by seat reservation schemes and by fares policy, as is the custom with airline services.

Stopping-Train Services

As a group, stopping-trains serve the more rural communities by linking small towns and villages with each other and, sometimes rather indirectly, with one or more major towns.

They merge into semi-fast services at one end of the range, where some semi-fast services could equally well be defined as stopping services, having regard to the traffic potential of the places where they stop as well as to their spacing. At the other end of the range, they merge very much further into suburban services. A suburban service has many of the characteristics of a stopping service, and is distinguished mainly by the intensity of its daily commuter peaks.

Railway stopping services developed as the predominant form of rural public transport service in the last century, when the only alternative was the horse-drawn vehicle and when the availability of private transport of any kind was very limited. Even in those days, when there was no satisfactory alternative and when fares were the present-day equivalent of 4½d. per mile third class, many of these services failed to pay.

Today, rail stopping services and bus services serve the same basic purpose. Buses carry the greater part of the passengers moving by public transport in rural areas, and, as well as competing with each other, both forms of public transport are fighting a losing battle against private transport.

15

Immediately prior to the war, in 1938, the number of private cars registered was 1,944,000. In 1954 there were 3,100,000, and in 1961 there were 6,000,000. By 1970 it is expected that there will be a total of 13,000,000 cars registered, equivalent to 24·3 per 100 of the population or 76 per 100 families. In addition, in 1961 there were 1,900,000 power-driven cycles of one kind or another.

Ownership of private transport is as common in rural areas as in towns. For example, the ownership of cars in the north of Scotland is 11·7 per 100 of the population, which equals the national average.

It is questionable whether British Railways meet as much as 10 per cent. of the total and declining demand for public rural transport. To do so, they provide services accounting for about 40 per cent. of the total passenger train mileage of the railways as a whole, and most of the trains carry an average of less than a bus-load and lose nearly twice as much as they collect in fares.

A high proportion of stopping-train services run over routes on which they provide the only form of rail passenger service, and on which the total traffic density is very low. Almost without exception, lines shown dotted or dashed in the passenger density map, i.e. lines carrying less than 5,000 or 10,000 passengers per week, are used for a single stopping service of passenger trains and for light flows of freight.

The economics of these lightly loaded passenger services can best be illustrated by an example.

Consider a single track route with small stations at intervals of 2½ miles carrying a stopping passenger service of one train per hour in each direction from 7.0 a.m. to 10.0 p.m. Irrespective of the number of passengers carried, typical costs will be:—

	Per mile per annum	Per mile per week
	£	£
System cost		
Route maintenance and signalling cost	3,000	58
Cost of stations (£2,500 per annum per station)	1,000	19
		77
Movement cost		
224 trains per week		
Steam locomotive hauled trains—about 15s. 0d. per train mile		168
Diesel multiple units — 4s. 0d. – 6s. 0d. per train mile according to density of traffic		45–67
Total cost of diesel multiple unit service		122–144
Revenue at 2d. per passenger mile		
1,000 passengers per week		8
2,500 passengers per week		21
5,000 passengers per week		42
7,500 passengers per week		63
10,000 passengers per week		83
15,000 passengers per week		125
20,000 passengers per week		167

Even with relatively low cost diesel multiple unit trains there will be losses up to quite high levels of traffic. This is illustrated in the following table which also includes a comparison with a bus service:—

Margins of Revenue over Costs for Low Density Passenger Flows

Traffic density passenger miles per route mile	DIESEL MULTIPLE UNIT TRAINS				BUS SERVICE	
	Margin over movement cost per mile		Margin over total cost (A) per mile	Margin over total cost (B) per mile	Margin over cost per mile (C)	
					Hourly service	Two-hourly service
	Per week	Per annum	Per annum	Per annum	Per annum	Per annum
	£	£	£	£	£	£
1,000	− 37	−1,900	−3,700	−5,900	−1,000	− 300
2,000	− 28	−1,500	−3,300	−5,500	− 600	+ 100
3,000	− 20	−1,000	−2,800	−5,000	− 200	+ 600
4,000	− 12	− 600	−2,400	−4,600	+ 300	
5,000	− 8	− 400	−2,200	−4,400	+ 700	
6,000	..	..	−1,800	−4,000		
7,000	+ 8	+ 400	−1,400	−3,600		
8,000	+ 17	+ 900	− 900	−3,100		
9,000	+ 25	+1,300	− 500	−2,700		
10,000	+ 33	+1,700	− 100	−2,300		
15,000	+ 66	+3,400	+1,600	− 600		
20,000	+100	+5,200	+3,400	+1,200		

(A) System cost attributable to passenger operation only charged assuming profitable freight absorbs the rest.

(B) Whole system cost charged assuming passenger traffic only on the route.

(C) This relates to a bus service receiving the same revenue as on rail, and bus operation at 2s. 6d. per mile.

These figures serve to show that the revenue earned from up to 6,000 passengers per week is unlikely to be sufficient to cover movement costs alone. This means that money would be saved by discontinuing such a service, even if the route continued to be maintained at its full level of cost for the sake of other traffic. In general, however, the presence of passenger traffic on even a single track branch line adds about £1,750 per mile per annum to the cost of maintaining and signalling the route, and of manning stations. Therefore, even where there is freight traffic capable of absorbing a share of the route cost, stopping passenger services cannot be regarded as paying their full cost below a passenger density of about 10,000. Where there is no other traffic, routes carrying up to 17,000 passengers per week may barely pay their way.

Although a high proportion of passenger services operate over lines of low total traffic density, there are also a considerable number of similar services operating over more densely loaded routes. In most cases, these services are just as unsound, financially, as those operating over branch lines. Below about 6,000 passenger miles per mile per week they do not pay for their own movement costs, even with short diesel multiple unit trains. Also, just as on branch lines, the presence of a stopping passenger service on a main line adds appreciably to the system cost, by complicating the signalling, and by necessitating the provision and manning of small stations. To be truly self-supporting, therefore,

17

they must be capable of covering system costs amounting to £1,000/2,000 per mile, and must carry around 10,000 passengers per week if they are to do so.

Confronted with evidence that a rail service does not pay, many people ask:—

(a) Why not decrease fares and attract more traffic?
(b) Why not give people the opportunity to pay higher fares and preserve the service?
(c) Why not substitute rail buses for trains and decrease the cost of the service?
(d) Why not run fewer trains?
(e) Why not close some stations?

Common-sense considerations, and all experience, go to show that the problem cannot be solved either by decreasing or increasing fares.

If fares were halved, traffic would have to increase at least fourfold to cover the direct costs of stopping services as a group, and sixfold to make them pay their whole costs. Nobody can seriously suppose that this would happen. People without their own transport, at present, are not so seriously deterred by the rail fares for short journeys that they would use trains many times as often if fares were halved.

To cover the costs of many services, fares would have to be increased to about eight or ten times their present level, even if traffic remained at its present density. It would, of course, disappear completely.

The third suggestion, that rail buses should be substituted for trains, ignores the high cost of providing the route itself, and also ignores the fact that rail buses are more expensive vehicles than road buses. The extent to which the economics remain unsound can readily be seen by inserting a Movement cost of three shillings per mile in the table on page 17. It would still be necessary to have a passenger density of 14,000 per week, to cover the total cost of the service, as compared with 17,000 per week with diesel multiple units. It is not immediately apparent either, why it is thought that rail buses would give a better standard of service than a road bus in most rural areas.

Similarly, consideration of the cost figures will show that thinning out the trains, or thinning out the stations, would not make a service self-supporting even if it had no adverse effect on revenue.

These points have been mentioned, to dispose of any idea that stopping-train services could be preserved, as an economic alternative to buses or private transport, if only some ingenuity were shown by railway operators. This really is not so, and it is obvious that a high proportion of stopping passenger train services ought to be discontinued as soon as possible, and that many of the lightly loaded lines over which they operate ought to close as well unless they carry exceptional freight traffic. For this reason, all stopping services have been examined individually, and so have all lengths of lightly loaded route.

So far as the services themselves are concerned, closure proposals have been determined by the inability of the services to produce revenue sufficient to cover the direct costs of operating them. Examples illustrative of this financial test are given in Appendix 2.

There can be no doubt about the financial desirability of closing those services which do not meet this test, and it is the Railways' wish to close them as soon as the procedure permits. Questions of hardships will be considered by the Transport Users Consultative Committees.

18

A list of services included in this group is given in Appendix 2. They account for an annual train mileage of 68 m. and the route mileage to be closed to passenger traffic will be about 5,000.

The savings expected to result from these withdrawals are £33 m. per annum and the loss of revenue is expected to be £15 m. per annum (£12 m. in earnings on the services concerned and £3 m. in contributory revenue), yielding a net improvement of £18 m. per annum excluding track and signalling. There will also be further savings, when lines are completely closed after withdrawal of passenger services and when alternative arrangements have been made to deal with any desirable freight. In large part, these savings are attributable to passenger service withdrawals. So also are the economies which will follow as the administrative and service departments are contracted and reorganised.

The stations affected by the closure of passenger services are listed in Appendix 2 and details of rolling stock which will be rendered redundant are given in Appendix 3.

Decision with regard to the remaining stopping services will be reserved for the present, until the most hopelessly uneconomic ones have been dealt with, but they will then be reviewed and should they be found to be uneconomic they will be dealt with similarly.

Hardship

It would be folly to suggest that widespread closure of stopping train services will cause no hardship anywhere or to anybody, and the Transport Act, 1962 makes the consideration of hardship the special responsibility of Transport Users Consultative Committees, where objections to closures are lodged. For the purpose of judging the closure proposals as a whole, however, it is necessary to have some idea of the scale and degree of hardship which they are likely to cause.

With the exception of northern Scotland, and parts of central Wales, most areas of the country are already served by a network of bus services more dense than the network of rail services which will be withdrawn, and in the majority of cases these buses already carry the major proportion of local traffic. With minor exceptions, these bus services cater for the same traffic flows as the railways, on routes which are roughly parallel. Taken as a whole, they have enough spare capacity to absorb the traffic which will be displaced from the railways, which will do no more than replace the bus traffic which has been lost over the last decade, and which will provide a very welcome addition to the revenue of the bus operators. The network of bus services is shown on Map No. 12.

In all these areas, cases of special difficulty will be rare, but there may be localities where there is not already a bus service connecting places at present served by rail. If the traffic displaced from rail has a density of over 1,000 passengers per week it provides the basis for an economic bus service of about eight buses each way. Where the traffic displaced is less than 1,000 passengers per week, and where a bus service does not exist already, some special arrangements may be necessary. Roughly a quarter of the services proposed for closure have a traffic density below 1,000, but it is estimated that only 122 miles of these routes are not already paralleled by bus services. In most areas of the country, therefore, it appears that hardship will arise on only a very limited scale.

19

In parts of Scotland, in particular, and to a lesser degree in Wales and the West country, road improvement or road construction may be necessary before adequate road services can be provided as full alternatives to the rail services which exist at present. Some of these road improvements are required, in any case, for development of the motor tourist trade, on which the future of these areas so greatly depends.

Suburban Services

The feature which distinguishes suburban services from a railway point of view, apart from the obvious fact that they are in suburban areas, is the intensity of the peaks caused by the daily movement of population in and out of focal cities. The other feature which distinguishes them in practice, though not of necessity, is a sub-normal level of fares.

The location of suburban services is made readily visible on the passenger traffic density map by the thickening of the lines in the vicinity of a few of the larger cities. London is the centre of a preponderant proportion of all such services in the country, and the characteristic morning and evening peaking of traffic intensity is more pronounced there than anywhere else. Outside London, there are only eight areas in which rail services are major contributors to the total daily flux of people in and out of the focal cities, these being Glasgow, Edinburgh, Newcastle, Manchester, Liverpool, Leeds, Birmingham and Cardiff.

To a greater or lesser degree, the pattern of life in all these areas is dependent upon continued operation of the suburban rail services, and to the life of London they are essential. It is, therefore, unthinkable to most people that these services might be closed, but that is no reason why they should be provided below cost.

In 1961, suburban services as a whole produced a gross revenue of £39·8 m. which was just less than their direct costs, and fell short of covering their total costs by £25 m. It is, however, misleading to consider all the services together, because conditions vary appreciably from area to area, and the London group of services is not only predominant in size but also presents problems of a distinctive kind.

London Services

London services, which earned £33 m. in 1961, or 86 per cent. of the total suburban services revenue, came near to covering their full cost. Nevertheless, their financial position, and the fares structure which gives rise to it, are highly unsatisfactory in relation to the traffic and operating problems which confront them. Strenuous efforts are being made to reduce the operating costs of these services, but it is abundantly clear that the scope for such reduction is inadequate to allow the matter to be put right by cost savings alone.

In essence, the problem is this. The capacity of the system carrying these services is limited by physical restrictions, particularly at the London end where so many services converge, and these restrictions could be removed only at very high cost. Many services are already saturated at peak hours, to the point where passengers suffer extreme discomfort, and the volume of traffic continues to rise. The level of fares is too low to finance costly increases in system capacity, but the demand goes on getting heavier.

This is a situation which must be of very real concern to the public, as well as to the railways, and it cannot be in the best interests of either to restrict fares to the low levels at which they are at present controlled.

There is also another feature which is important from a commercial point of view. The rail system is capable of drawing passengers travelling daily to London from distances up to a hundred miles, and has ample spare capacity for doing so beyond a radius of about 20 miles. It is, therefore, in the railways' interest to foster growth of this longer distance traffic to achieve higher utilisation of the route system as a whole, but this development is itself restricted by the congestion of shorter distance traffic at the London end.

The magnitude of the morning and evening traffic peaks is illustrated by figures showing the flow through some of the main London terminals at various hours of the day.

The peak load, measured over half an hour, is about 10 times the average level over the hours from 6 a.m. to midnight, and 12 times the average over 24 hours. The route and rolling stock capacity provided to deal with the peak is used to only 10 per cent. of its capacity during the hours over which it might normally be expected to carry passengers, and to 8½ per cent. capacity over the whole day. In spite of this, practically the whole peak traffic is carried at reduced rates. Also, and more logically, cheap fares are offered during off-peak periods in an effort to attract traffic when it can be carried at low marginal cost, so that nearly all the traffic is carried at low rates for one reason or another.

The effective level of fares for London suburban service traffic, and the growth of traffic over the years is demonstrated by the following table:—

BRITISH RAILWAYS—LONDON LINES

Estimated average receipt per mile, passenger journeys and passenger miles

Year	Estimated average receipt per mile		Estimated passenger journeys		Estimated passenger miles	
	All	Season tickets only	All	Season tickets only	All	Season tickets only
	d.	*d.*	*m.*	*m.*	*m.*	*m.*
1949	1·01	0·77	N.A.	N.A.	4,643	N.A.
1954	1·17	0·94	493	175	4,579	2,083
1955	1·26	1·00	478	170	4,437	2,027
1956	1·31	1·03	491	190	4,677	2,280
1957	1·33	1·06	504	203	4,875	2,435
1958	1·43	1·14	527	201	4,865	2,385
1959	1·44	1·16	507	206	4,836	2,437
1960	1·63	1·33	497	202	4,731	2,384
1961	1·74	1·39	501	206	4,880	2,550

1955 .. .. A.S.L.E. & F. strike from 20th May to 14th June.

End of 1956 and early 1957 .. Suez crisis.

1958 .. .. L.T.E. bus strike 5th May to 20th June.

It should be clearly recognised that the problem presented by the London suburban rail services is not one which the railways can solve alone. Their problem is part of the whole problem of London congestion, and measures which would improve their situation, such as staggering of hours and dispersal of employment to the periphery of the metropolitan area, are beyond their power and responsibility. Also, unless the control of fares in the London Traffic Area is exercised with more regard to the true nature of the problem, the position will be further worsened by the continued suppression of normal economic forces.

Suburban Services Outside London

No city other than London is nearly so predominantly dependent upon suburban train services. All of them are served by public road transport which carries a high proportion of the total daily flow, and the movement and parking of private transport is still sufficiently free to make it a possible alternative to rail. Also, none of the services is loaded as heavily as many London services.

As in the case of London, fares on these services feeding other cities are low, sometimes very low, and none of them pays its way. There is no possibility of a solution being found, however, merely by increasing or by reducing fares. Increases in fares on rail services alone would drive traffic to available alternative modes of travel and yield little increase in revenue, if any. Decreases would increase traffic, but short peak periods of traffic at even saturation level would not support the services with fares lower than at present. Therefore, if the services are to be regarded as essential, the municipalities concerned must join with the railways and bus interests to evolve a co-ordinated system of services, with due regard to the economics of both forms of transport. It is, for example, illogical to operate subsidised municipal bus services in competition with unprofitable railway services, without any attempt to co-ordinate them.

If, on the other hand, the services are not regarded as essential and co-ordination is not found possible, the sound commercial course is for the railways to risk pricing themselves out of the business and then, if necessary, close the services.

The right solution is most likely to be found by 'Total Social Benefit Studies' of the kind which are now being explored by the Ministry of Transport and British Railways jointly. In cases of the type under consideration it may be cheaper to subsidise the railways than to bear the other cost burdens which will arise if they are closed. If this happens, however, there should be no feeling that the railways are being propped up by such a subsidy because of a commercial failure.

Mails and Parcels

The regular passenger train services are the principal means of conveyance for Post Office parcels and letter mails, as well as for the railways' own parcels service.

Schedules of services, agreed with the Post Office, are laid down for the conveyance of the majority of letter mails, and extend over seven days of the week. Also, Post Office letter sorting vehicles run nightly on some routes, the average number per week being 80. Letter mails are loaded into and unloaded from train vans by Post Office staff, and are transferred by them at intermediate stations if necessary.

Post Office parcels are mainly carried on passenger trains, but are loaded and unloaded by railway staff.

The railway itself accepts, collects and delivers parcels for carriage by passenger trains, or by booked special parcels trains, during normal business hours on six days of the week. A countrywide service is available to and from all stations open to passengers, and also to some stations which were formerly served by passenger trains but are no longer. No extra charge is normally made for collection and delivery, although extra charges are now raised in a few areas where conditions are exceptional.

Facilities for trunk conveyance of parcels and mails will improve with the improvement of main line services, but withdrawals of stopping services will reduce the number of places which can be served by rail movement throughout. No great volume of traffic will be affected, and the problems which will arise are being considered with the Post Office.

Another, and very important problem which concerns both the Post Office and British Railways is the overlapping of their parcels services, on which both organisations lose money.

The Post Office gives a nation-wide service for parcels up to 22 lb. in weight, and with fairly tight restriction on size. They do not collect parcels, except for their own convenience, but they do deliver.

The railways accept parcels up to 2 cwt. in weight, without any limitation on size or shape. They collect and deliver the parcels, provide evidence of delivery if necessary, and compensate for loss or damage.

In 1961 the railways handled 50 m. bags of parcels post for the Post Office, estimated to contain 255 m. parcels of average weight 5 lb., and yielding receipts of £30 m. to the Post Office, of which the railways received £12 m.

The railways carried 84 m. consignments in their own parcels service in 1961, with receipts of £27 m. This traffic, like Post Office parcels traffic, has shown a rising trend in recent years.

An analysis of the railways' service in 1960 shows that 3,368 of the smaller stations produced only 4 per cent. of the receipts from parcels and miscellaneous traffic by coaching train. At the other end of the scale, 22 stations accounted for 45 per cent. of the total receipts. As might be expected, this railways parcels traffic, and Post Office parcels traffic, is distributed over the country in much the same pattern as wagon load and sundries freight traffic.

The Post Office are reported to lose £8·4 m. on their parcels service, and the railways passenger parcels traffic makes an inadequate contribution to system cost. To a considerable degree the two forms of service compete for traffic which is not favourable to either, and render it even less so by the duplication of facilities where both are little used. In addition, they also compete with road parcels services, in particular with British Road Services, but road operators limit their coverage to the more remunerative areas.

Co-ordination of services and charging scales are the subject of active discussions between the Post Office and the railways, and problems arising from railway closures will be treated as part of the broader problem. These discussions will also embrace consideration of better means of handling mails and parcels at terminals.

Reference will be made to possible amalgamation of some parts of the parcel service with freight sundries traffic in a later section.

23

FREIGHT TRAFFIC

Consideration of freight traffic is all important to the future of the railways as a nation-wide system. Without freight the main railway network could not exist. Although passenger trains can be operated profitably over main routes where they have to contribute only a part of the route cost, they would, on their own, be capable of supporting only a small fraction of the existing route mileage outside the London suburban area. It is encouraging to see, therefore, how well freight traffic is spread over all the routes on which passenger train services are likely to continue.

It can be seen, by comparing the freight density map with the passenger density map, that practically all routes which carry over 10,000 passengers a week, carry at least 10,000 tons of freight. It is evident, too, that a very high proportion of lines which are dotted or dashed on the passenger map, i.e. lines over which passenger services are normally found to be uneconomic, are also shown dotted, as very low density lines, on the freight map. Provided the general level of freight business can be built up, therefore, there is promise that freight and passenger traffics will prove mutually supporting over most of that half of the total route mileage which carries 95 per cent. of all traffic at present, while very little freight or passenger traffic will be lost if most of the remainder is closed.

The possibility of generating and handling more remunerative freight traffic is of key importance. Before we turn to that subject, however, some attention must be given to the present method of freight handling on the railways, because success in attracting traffic and making it remunerative will depend upon improvements in the system of moving it.

Present Method of Handling Freight Traffic

Whereas all passengers move on services which can be individually distinguished and identifiably associated with particular routes, this is not so with most freight. Some freight traffic is carried by through trains, but the greater part of it moves quite differently, by a system which can best be understood in the light of its history.

Our railways were developed to their fullest extent at a time when the horse and cart were the only means of feeding to and distributing from them. Therefore, as the railways grew, because of the deficiencies of horse transport on poor roads, the main network of routes was extended by an even closer network of branches, with close spacing of stations over the whole system, in order to reduce road movement to a minimum. Because of this penetration of rail movement so far into the stages of collection and delivery, and the associated multiplicity of stations and depots, a great deal of traffic originated and terminated in single wagon load consignments.

Over the same era, there was a linking of the mainline railways into a national network, with an enormous increase in the number of places to which traffic originating in any one place might be consigned. As a result, the wagon became the unit of movement and through working of trains was largely suppressed. Instead, nearly all freight moved by the staging of wagons from marshalling yard to marshalling yard, with variable and cumulative delays in them, so that the overall journey was bound to be slow and unpredictable.

24

Thus, in order to provide for a large measure of rail participation in country-wide collection and delivery of small consignments, which the railways were never particularly well suited to do, and which they only did because the horse-drawn cart was worse, the railways threw away their main advantages. They saddled themselves with the costly movement of wagons in small numbers over a multiplicity of branch lines, where there were too few wagons moving to make good trains. At the same time, they sacrificed the speed, reliability, and low cost of through-train operation even on the main arteries.

This staging of wagons is carried out in accordance with a set of rules, but these rules, like those of chess, allow a considerable variation of speed and route for a transit between any two points. To a large extent, therefore, we are compelled to think of the system of freight movement as one which produces statistically measurable and predictable results, but which does not produce a known or foreseeable result with any one consignment.

The slow and semi-random movement of wagons, and their dispersal over many small terminals where they cannot be collected or delivered very frequently, has necessitated the provision of an enormous fleet of wagons. Also, because of their random motion, all these wagons have to be capable of coupling and running with one another and of going almost anywhere on the system. This compatibility requirement, combined with the size and cost of the fleet, has been a great obstacle to technical progress, since the new always has to mate with the old. In consequence, evolution of improved rolling stock has been very slow.

The average turn-round time between loading and loading for British Railways' wagons is 11·9 working days. The average loaded transit time is about $1\frac{1}{2}$–2 days, with an average journey length of 67 miles, but individual transit times are bound to vary over a wide range, not merely because of variations in distance but also because of variations in route and in marshalling delays.

These slow and variable delivery times are quite unacceptable for many forms of freight in these days, when road deliveries over comparable distances can be made on the day of despatch. In addition, however, this whole method of rail movement by the staging of wagons is far more costly than movement by through trains.

As we shall see later, the way to break with the past is not to attempt an overall change of the present system but to develop new services, with new rolling stock not compatible with the old, which will progressively displace the common-user wagon fleet and the system of operation which employs it.

The Main Classes of Freight Traffic

Reference has already been made to the main classes into which freight traffic is traditionally divided.

They are:

(i) Coal class traffic, which includes coal, coke, and manufactured solid fuels.

(ii) Mineral traffic, a more mixed class, which includes true mineral traffics such as iron ore, limestone, china clay, etc., but which also includes steel industry semi-finished products, ashes, iron and steel scrap, bricks, creosote and tar, fertilizer, and even sugar beet.

(iii) General merchandise, also covers a very wide range of commodities, as its name implies, and the bulk of it is made up of manufactured products of many kinds.

Consignment sizes in this class of traffic vary enormously and, for practical reasons, the broad class is sub-divided into two groups according to whether consignments are large enough to make a wagon-load or not.

As already mentioned, only one of the three main classes of freight is profitable and the 1961 results were:—

Class of traffic	Tons	Receipts	Margin of receipts over direct cost	Estimated margin over total cost
	m.	*£m.*	*£m.*	*£m.*
Coal	145·7	108·3	24·8	2·8
Mineral	54·3	44·5	7·6	− 3·7
General merchandise:				
Wagon-load ..	34·4 } 38·2	64·8 } 102·8	−31·8 } −45·3	−53·8 } −75·1
Sundries	3·8	38·0	−13·5	−21·3

The trends in volume and receipts for these classes of traffic over recent years are shown by Figures Nos. 1, 2 and 3.

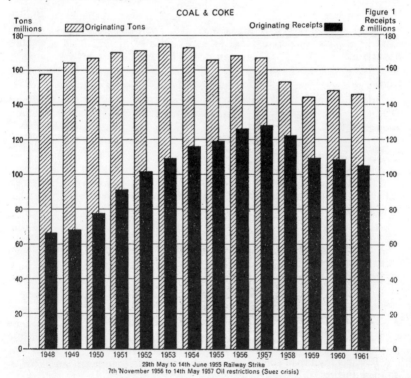

COAL & COKE

Figure 1

29th May to 14th June 1955 Railway Strike
7th November 1956 to 14th May 1957 Oil restrictions (Suez crisis)

26

MINERALS

Figure 2

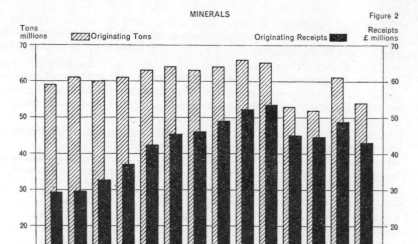

29th May to 14th June 1955 Railway Strike
7th November 1956 to 14th May 1957 Oil restrictions (Suez crisis)

GENERAL MERCHANDISE

Figure 3

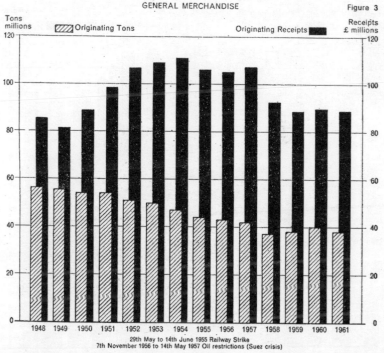

29th May to 14th June 1955 Railway Strike
7th November 1956 to 14th May 1957 Oil restrictions (Suez crisis)

Receipts from road conveyance and miscellaneous sources are not included in these Figures.

27

The great significance of these figures is underlined by the realisation that the only traffic which the railways can hope to carry in much larger volume in future is general merchandise.

The total ton mileage of coal traffic is more likely to decrease than increase, and since the railways are already the predominant carriers of coal, they have only limited scope for increasing their share of the total. Bulk mineral traffic is likely to increase in tonnage with growth of the economy, but ton mileage is unlikely to increase very fast. Again, since the railways already carry a very high proportion of the total traffic of this kind, any increase in their share can only be small. By contrast, the railways are the minority carriers of general merchandise and that part of the mineral class of traffic which is of like character. Also, this kind of traffic is certain to grow in volume, at least as fast as the general growth in the economy. This, therefore, is the type of traffic which offers the railways the best opportunity for increasing their freight loadings.

Of recent years, however, the railways' share of this traffic has declined and, at present, it is a serious loss maker. Therefore, the railways are confronted with the twofold task of making such radical changes in the handling of this traffic as to render it profitable and of attracting more of it. Fortunately, methods of handling are envisaged which will give a much more satisfactory quality of service at costs substantially below competitive rates.

This will be considered further in the section dealing with general merchandise freight. First, however, something must be said about coal and mineral traffics.

Coal Traffic

There are 620 collieries in Great Britain and 600 are rail connected. The output is distributed by rail, sea, road, and waterways, or by a combination of some of these means.

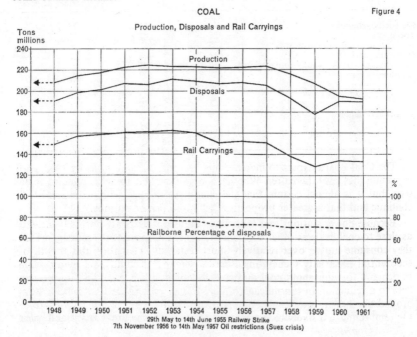

COAL   Figure 4

Production, Disposals and Rail Carryings

29th May to 14th June 1955 Railway Strike
7th November 1956 to 14th May 1957 Oil restrictions (Suez crisis)

Over a period of years the total production of coal has declined and, until recently, the proportion carried by rail has also fallen. The trends are shown in Figure No. 4.

The growth of road transport has been responsible for the decline in the railways' share of the traffic, and in 1961 the total tonnage forwarded by the National Coal Board was spread over the main forms of transport as shown below:—

				Million tons
Rail	..	..	..	133
Road	..	..	..	39
Private line	..	..	9
Canal	..	..	..	3
Other	..	..	..	5
TOTAL	..	..	189

Twenty-two million tons carried by rail, private line and canal to shipping points was subsequently carried by coastwise vessels.

The volume and geographical distribution of coal flows by sea and road during 1960 is shown in Map No. 6.

Trends in the pattern of consumption of coal also affect the transport problem, and figures below show how the pattern has changed between 1956 and 1961 and how it is likely to change over the next five years.

Million Tons

	1956	1961	1966
Electricity generation	46·3	55·4	75·5
Towns gas	28·1	22·5	16·5
Iron and steel and coke ovens	36·3	31·2	30
Other industrial	34·2 ⎫	26·3 ⎫	23·5 ⎫
Household coal and naturally smokeless fuels	32·9 ⎬106·8	28·9 ⎬82·7	27 ⎬71
All other	39·7 ⎭	27·5 ⎭	20·5 ⎭
	217·5	191·8	193
Export and bunkers	9·7	5·7	7
TOTAL	227·2	197·5	200

The Coal Board expect to increase their output to 200 m. tons by 1966, and to sustain that level thereafter. Whether they will be able to do so remains to be seen, but it is almost certain that the change of pattern within the total will continue and that a greater proportion will go to power stations.

Because power stations and other large industrial users are normally located as close to coal fields as other considerations permit, most of the tonnage which they consume moves over relatively short distances. Therefore, the growth of the Central Electricity Generating Board's demand, accompanied by a decline in demand for household coal and coal for many other small consumers, will lead to a reduction in ton-mileage of coal traffic, even if the total output stays around the 200 m. tons level. For that reason, although the railways' share of the total tonnage is likely to increase to some extent, the ton-mileage and gross revenue will fall. It does not follow, however, that the net revenue will also decrease, because there will be a higher proportion of bulk movement which is favourable to rail.

In 1961, the rail coal traffic which totalled 146 m. tons was spread over the main consumer groups as shown below:—

Rail Carryings of Coal Class Traffic (1961)

Consumer	m. tons
C.E.G.B.	30·7
Gas	11·0
Blast furnaces ..	18·0
Other industrial ..·	22·3
Shipment	22·9
Domestic	27·6
Balance*	13·2
TOTAL ..	145·7

* Balance mainly accounted for by coal to washeries, for stocking, and hauled by Coal Board locomotives over British Railways' system.

A high proportion of the coal for large consumers already moves by through-train operation and 57 m. tons, or 39 per cent. of the 1961 total was moved in that way, while the remainder moved by the wagon-load. Of the 89 m. tons which moved by the staging of wagons, 54 m. went to private sidings and 35 m. tons went to stations.

Movement of coal by through-train operation enables greater benefit to be derived from the potential advantages of rail transport than does single wagon movement. Even with this type of traffic, however, terminal conditions and established practices militate against really economic use of rail facilities. As a result, there has been some erosion of bulk flows of coal by road competitors, in spite of the very substantial cost advantage which rail is potentially able to give.

The main trouble arises at the collieries, for a combination of reasons which spring from the histories of the two industries. First, there are few collieries which produce enough coal of any one type to supply a large consumer, so that the flow to, say, a large generating station has to be built up by drawing from a group of them. A second and even more serious difficulty is that none of the collieries has storage bunkers and facilities for rapid loading of trains, although quite a number of them are able to load road vehicles without delay, from elevated hoppers. Instead, the collieries use railway wagons as bunkers and need to have a large supply of them available for that purpose at all times. As a result, wagons spend an average of 2 days in colliery sidings, and, at present, the Coal Board pay practically nothing for their use during that time.

The total annual cost of providing wagons for coal traffic exceeds the total haulage cost and is about £30 m. a year. The Coal Board have the use of them as bunkers for about 22 million wagon days a year, either at pits or washeries. This, with an allowance for coverage of peak demands, costs the railways about £1 for each wagon supplied, or about £11 m. per year. Under established practice, the Coal Board pay a total demurrage charge of only £1 m. per annum.

It is true that a charge of 2s. 6d. per ton is made to road hauliers by the Coal Board to cover the cost of landsale facilities, and this may be regarded as offsetting the cost to the railways of supplying wagons, but there are two important differences. The road haulier only pays when he moves coal, while the railways have to bear the cost of wagon provision even when the wagons are not in full use. Also, the facility for which the road operator pays is one which is designed to meet his need for quick loading. The railways, on the other hand, do not, in many cases, have their requirements met by being provided with complete trainloads ready for haulage to a single destination as a return to them for the cost of having made wagons available at pits. It should be said, however, that the staff at many pits do help in this respect when they can.

A rather similar situation often exists at the receiving end where wagons are again used for storage while road vehicles are emptied at once. The position is especially bad at the ports.

The degree to which the position is unsatisfactory is made more apparent when consideration is given to the supply to new power stations. To take advantage of new locomotives and make the rail haul more efficient, the sound course is to use large, braked, hopper wagons, which have a better load/tare weight ratio, which can be drawn at high speed, and which can be unloaded very quickly at the receiving terminal. Such wagons are relatively costly, but are much more economical to use if they can be turned round quickly. They are, however, too expensive to be used as storage bunkers at the pits, and need to be loaded quickly from static bunkers.

The Coal Board show understanding of the railways' problem, but it is very understandable that they do not voluntarily spend money for the purpose of providing bunkerage and train loading facilities at pits, all the while the railways provide wagons for use as bunkers without charge. To bring about provision of loading bunkers, and cover the railways' cost of wagoning the pits in the meanwhile, it will be necessary to charge the Coal Board the full cost of wagons retained by them. At present, however, trains of new wagons, capable of making several round trips per day, are being limited to one trip every 2½ to 3 days by the absence of quick loading facilities at the pits.

Although the cost of through-train movement of coal is higher than it need be because of terminal conditions, the cost of moving it in single wagon loads to stations and sidings for small consumers is very much higher still. Over a hundred-mile haul, for example, the movement cost is about twice as great, and typical figures for the two different types of movement are shown on the following page. System cost is not included.

31

Estimated Direct Costs for a Transit of 100 miles

	(a) Single wagon consignment (16-*ton capacity wagon*) from colliery to small station on branch line	(b) Through-train load consignment (16-*ton capacity wagons*) *from colliery to private siding*
	Per wagon	Per wagon
	s.	s.
(1) Terminal facilities and services at both ends of transit; documentation	96 (including local trip working to first, and from last marshalling yard)	28
(2) Provision of wagon ..	92	32
(3) Marshalling	21	..
(4) Trunk haul	69 (85 miles)	93 (100 miles)
Total	278	153
Cost per ton (14·5 tons per wagon)	19·0	10·6

Since 61 per cent. of the total coal moved by the railways is still handled by wagon-load movement, at correspondingly high costs, it is very necessary to consider what can be done to enable more of it to be handled in through-trains. In this connection, the data given in Appendix 1 is of particular interest. This shows how the total 28·1 m. tons received by stations was spread over the 5,031 stations open to coal traffic in 1960. Although open to receive coal, 1,172 stations received none and many of these have obviously fallen into disuse for this purpose. A further 1,790 received between one and five wagons per week and totalled only 1·7 m. tons between them in the year, or 6 per cent. of the whole. At the other end of the scale 64 stations received over 50,000 tons per year each, and between them received 20 per cent. of the total. In between, 2,005 stations, receiving 2,500 to 50,000 tons/year each, together accounted for 74 per cent. of the total.

All the coal from these stations is distributed by road in any case, with an average radius of distribution of 2½ miles at present. Since the whole country can be covered by a 10-mile radius of distribution from 250 centres, the costs of road distribution would not be greatly increased by reducing the number of rail-served coal depots to a few hundred large ones which could be supplied by through-train movement. The resulting reduction in rail costs would be very considerable, and depots large enough to be fed by the train-load would also have enough throughput to justify efficient mechanisation and the use of special purpose road vehicles, so that the overall cost of handling and distribution from depots could be reduced as well.

Even in the absence of improved facilities and practices at the pits, rail costs could be reduced by about 6s. per ton on the average length of haul, and if the pits consigned coal to depots in train-load quantities, so as to eliminate the initial rail collection and marshalling, a further 1s. 6d. per ton could be saved on direct cost.

Such changes would be in the best interests of the Coal Board, the railways, and coal consumers, because the potential savings are large enough to improve the competitiveness of the first two and to give a worthwhile reduction in the delivered price of coal. For the same reason, the changes will be beneficial to the coal trade as a whole, but may not be welcomed by all individual merchants, especially some of the smaller ones.

A number of coal concentration depots of the type envisaged have already been established and schemes for others are being developed. It is very much in the interests of the railways to accelerate progress in this direction, but it would not be wise for them to provide the depots themselves. By doing so, they would commit themselves, even further than at present, to fixed investment in a business which they do not control. Therefore, although the railways will encourage and facilitate the establishment of concentration depots, they will not normally invest in them. They will, however, induce concentration by a rapid progressive closure of the smaller stations, a process which is also necessary on other grounds.

In this last connection it needs to be stressed, once again, that the cost figures quoted do not include system cost, and that this may be very great on lightly used branch lines where many of the smaller stations are to be found.

Mineral Traffic

For the purpose of the traffic studies, this mixed class of traffic was combined with general merchandise. Therefore, not a great deal need be said about it as a separate class.

As in the case of coal, a considerable proportion of this traffic, in particular that comprised of bulk minerals, is carried in block trains. The more hetero-geneous remainder is carried by wagon movement and is distinguishable from the greater part of general merchandise traffic only by rather arbitrary definitions. Since some of the freight classed as general merchandise also lends itself to bulk movement, there is little reason to treat the two classes separately for present purposes.

It is worth mentioning, however, that the movement of bulk minerals provides some of the best examples of really efficient use of rail transport. Some big flows are carried in large trains of special wagons, served through efficient terminals, and yield profits to the railways and very low freight rates to the customers. They serve to show what could be done with coal.

33

Wagon-Load Mineral and General Merchandise Freight Traffic

Under this heading is considered mineral and general merchandise traffic, other than general merchandise sundries. The description 'wagon-load' is not used here to distinguish between the through train and wagon forwarding modes of movement, but only to exclude consignments of less than a wagon load.

In 1961, this group of traffics as a whole, amounting to 89 m. tons, produced receipts of £109·3 m., but failed to cover its direct costs by £24·2 m. and fell short of covering its total costs by £57·5 m. It is, however, a very mixed class of traffic which not only includes a wide variety of commodities but which also covers a very wide range of all the other variables which determine the suitability of traffic for rail transport, such as terminal conditions, consignment size, loadability, length of haul, etc. It is, therefore, particularly necessary to analyse this group of traffics in detail to determine how much of it can be regarded as good rail traffic.

The commodity composition of the 89 m. tons of this traffic carried in 1961 is as follows :—

Mineral Traffic	Million Tons
Bricks, clay, common	1·1
Bricks, refractory	0·5
Clay, common or fire	0·4
Fertilisers and manure	2·0
Iron and steel, bars, billets, etc.	4·4
Iron and steel scrap	6·1
Iron ore	16·6
Iron, pig	2·6
Lime and limestone	7·4
O.T.W.—Bitumen, creosote, etc.	0·9
Roadstone	0·2
Sand, common	1·6
Slag, cinders and ashes	1·0
Sugar beet	1·0
Other	8·6
Total	54·4 (of which 23·2 m. tons, or 43 per cent. moved in full train loads)

	General Merchandise	*Million Tons*
Animal feeding stuffs	.. .. ..	1·3
Beer	.. ..	0·3
Butter, margarine, etc.	.. ..	0·2
Cement ..	.. ..	1·6
Chemicals, not in O.T.W.	.. ..	1·3
Confectionery ..	.. .. ..	0·8
Esparto grass and wood pulp	..	0·6
Fruit	.. ..:	0·5
Grain and flour	.. .. ..	1·4
Iron and steel—other products	..	8·6
Machinery	.. ..	0·4
Meat	.. ..	0·2
O.T.W.—chemicals	.. .. ..	1·0
O.T.W.—fuel and petrol	.. ..	4·8
O.T.W.—other	.. .. ..	0·4
Paper and cardboard ..	.. ..	0·6
Potatoes	.. ..	0·5
Soap and detergents	.. .. ..	0·2
Sugar	.. ..	0·3
Textiles and drapery ..	.. ..	0·1
Timber—pit props	.. .. ..	0·5
Timber—other	.. ..	0·9
Wines and spirits	.. .. ..	0·3
Wool	.. ..	0·1
Other	.. ..	7·5
TOTAL	..	34·4

34·4 (of which 6·5 m. tons, or 19 per cent. moved in full train loads)

O.T.W. = Owners' Tank Wagons.

It will be seen that 30 m. tons of the total of 89 m. tons in the group was carried in block trains, and virtually all of this moved from private siding to private siding, or between private siding and a dock. It is necessary to comment, however, that not all siding and dock traffic moves in train-load quantities.

One of the main objects of the freight traffic survey made over the test week, ending 23rd April, 1961, was to determine what proportions of traffic flowed between terminals of different kinds, how each of these groups was spread over different ranges of distance moved, how they varied in wagon loading, and how costs for the various groups compared with receipts. All this information is set out in Tables I to VI of Appendix 1.

The traffic surveyed in the test week amounted to 1,695,000 tons. This compared closely in volume with the weekly average for the whole year, although actual carryings, measured in terms of loaded wagons forwarded, were rather

35

below that level. The total costs shown for the week, for this reason, are also a little below the average. On the other hand, the receipts shown for the week are somewhat above average. To the extent of perhaps 5 per cent., this is due to insufficient allowance for outpayments, rebates and other adjustments in the calculation of the actual earnings for each individual consignment. The balance is attributable to the particular composition of the traffic during the test week.

It is inevitable that there is variation in the component traffics as between one period and another, and seasonal fluctuation, which affects some of the most important traffics, is not the least of the causes. Whilst the results shown in the Tables thus appear a little more favourable than the figures for the full year (which also include some receipts and costs from relatively small sources not included in the test), they are, nevertheless, sufficiently representative to constitute a most informative analysis of the traffic in this group.

One of the main subdivisions in the Tables is based upon terminal conditions, and this brings out very clearly the gross unprofitability of most station traffics and the relatively favourable nature of siding-to-siding movement. Thus:—

ANALYSIS BY TERMINAL CONDITIONS

Combination of terminal conditions. (Flow in either direction)	Tons	Per cent.	Receipts	Per cent.	Direct costs	Per cent.	Margin
			£		£		£
Road–Road ..	26,800	2	145,300	7	214,100	9	− 68,800
Road–Station ..	17,600	1	64,400	3	91,700	4	− 27,300
Road–Dock ..	25,400	1	61,600	3	91,900	4	− 30,300
Road–Siding ..	111,500	7	299,900	13	376,000	17	− 76,100
Station–Station..	30,200	2	66,300	3	91,800	4	− 25,500
Station–Dock ..	29,600	2	65,000	3	72,500	3	− 7,500
Dock–Dock ..	5,400	..	3,900	..	9,500	..	− 5,600
Station–Siding ..	246,600	14	369,500	16	379,600	17	− 10,100
Siding–Dock ..	256,300	15 ⎱71	190,500	8 ⎱52	200,900	9 ⎱42	− 10,400
Siding–Siding ..	946,000	56 ⎰	986,500	44 ⎰	746,200	33 ⎰	+240,300

One obvious feature is that any traffic which is road collected or delivered by the railways is carried at a heavy loss relative to direct costs. The high cost of collecting or delivering by road, plus the cost of hand transfer of freight between road and rail vehicles, makes it impossible to attract traffic at economic prices. As a result, the railways get practically none of the better loading traffic in this way, but are used for poor loading traffic which road hauliers would reject or carry only at very high prices. This view is confirmed by the very low wagon loads produced by this traffic, the average for road/road and road/station traffic being only 2·5 tons per wagon.

The railways' financial losses are much the same on traffic which passes through stations without road collection or delivery by the railways' own vehicles, because transfer and road movement is still necessary, and railway rates have to allow for this cost being borne by the customer. Consequently, as groups, station/station and station/dock traffics both show a loss relative to their direct costs, while station/siding traffics just about break even. Here, however, as in the case of other traffics, increases in wagon loading or in length of haul have a beneficial effect, and that part of the traffic in the last two terminal groups which loads best or travels furthest yields some margin over direct costs as a contribution to system costs.

In the non-station traffics, siding/dock traffic falls just short of paying its direct costs, while siding/siding traffic produces a good margin. These were the terminal combinations for 71 per cent. of all the traffic covered by the survey, of which siding/siding traffics alone accounted for 56 per cent.

These terminal conditions are particularly favourable to rail, because no transfers from vehicle to vehicle are involved, because they give rise to good loading traffics (12·3 tons/wagon), and because a high proportion of the traffic can be moved in trainload quantities. The test week tonnage of freight passing under these terminal conditions is equivalent to 62·5 m. tons/year, and, as has already been mentioned, about 30 m. tons of this is carried by through trains.

The figures as a whole make it very clear that the mineral and general merchandise traffic falls roughly into two main groups, distinguished by whether or not the traffic passes through a station at either end, these being:—

(1) Siding/siding or siding/dock traffic, nearly two-thirds of which moves in train-load quantities, which accounts for 71 per cent. of the total tonnage, and which, on the basis of the test week, appears to yield a margin over direct costs of about £12 m., p.a.

(2) Traffic which passes through a station at one or both ends of its transit, which is virtually all based upon wagon load movement with poor wagon loading, and which, on the basis of the test week, appears to give rise to a deficit relative to direct costs of £13 m., p.a.

Even in the non-station based group, not all traffic is good. As has already been mentioned, that which flows between sidings and docks falls just short of covering its costs, partly because a great deal of it is short haul traffic and partly because terminal conditions at docks often cause wagons to suffer long delays.

There is a lesser proportion of siding-to-siding traffic which moves under 25 miles, and the bulk of it is spread fairly evenly over haulage distances from 50 to 200 miles, with fairly good wagon loading for all distances. As will be seen from Table V of Appendix 1, however, about 5 per cent. of the siding-to-siding traffic which loads to less than 6 tons/wagon does not pay its way.

This light loading traffic is not necessarily associated with smaller sidings, although much of it is likely to be. Also, in general, costs of servicing small sidings are greater. It is, therefore, of interest to see, from Tables Nos. 19, 20 and 21 of Appendix 1, how unevenly traffic is spread over the total number of private sidings which exist. About 78 per cent. of all traffic flows through 855 of them, while a further 5,039 sidings account for only the remaining 22 per cent. of the total traffic.

In the station-based group of traffic there is practically none which is good, as handled at present, and most of it is extremely bad. Some of it is so bad that it may well be the right course for the railways to reject it in future, but first it is necessary to consider:—

(a) whether some of the traffic could be made profitable in future;

(b) whether some of it must be carried to give full service to important private siding customers;

(c) to what extent could expenses be saved if some or all of the traffic were not carried ?

These questions cannot easily be dealt with separately, and what follows has some bearing upon each of them.

It is noteworthy that of the 25·4 m. tons of traffic which the traffic test showed to pass through stations each year, 12·8 m. tons moved siding/station, and a further 5·8 m. tons moved siding/road. This is traffic which it is particularly necessary to consider in relation to (a) and (b) above.

The first of these groups of traffic only just about paid its direct costs in 1961, and, as will be seen later, it should be possible to move much of it in ways which will make it remunerative traffic. It will be noticed from Table V of Appendix 1, that a very high proportion of it gives good wagon loading, and it will also be found, later, that most of it moves between a relatively small number of large centres.

The smaller group of traffics which moves siding/road does not load so well, but about 70 per cent. makes wagon loads over 6 tons. It does, therefore, include a substantial proportion of potentially good traffic which, in common with that mentioned in the previous paragraph, will be referred to again in the section dealing with Liner Trains.

As might be expected, most of this siding/station traffic, whether it includes road movement or not, is a flow outwards from sidings to stations. This is confirmed by the marked disparity between the total of traffic received by stations during the test week and that forwarded, as shown by Tables Nos. 11 and 12 of Appendix 1. Traffic received exceeded forwardings by an annual rate of 9·3 m. tons which shows how preponderantly the flow of siding/station traffic must have been a flow out from sidings.

It has already been pointed out that a preponderance of the siding traffic passes through a relatively small proportion of the total number of private sidings which exist, and Table 18, which shows how traffic is spread over sidings grouped under parent stations, also makes it evident that sidings handling most of the traffic are concentrated in a few areas of high industrial or population density. It is equally evident from Tables 11 and 12, that most of the station traffic passes through a small proportion of the total number of stations, and that the siding/station traffic is mostly received by the large ones. The following figures illustrate this point:—

Stations forwarding or receiving less than 100 tons/week			Stations forwarding or receiving more than 100 tons/week		
Total received	Total forwarded	Difference	Total received	Total forwarded	Difference
'000 tons/week			'000 tons/week		
54·2	41·1	13·1	315·7	149·1	166·6

These points are of interest and importance in connection with the closure of small stations, since it appears that not only do such stations handle very little of the total volume of merchandise freight but, also, that what they do

38

handle must be predominantly of the very poor road/road, road/station or station/station types. Moreover, since so little siding/station traffic flows to such stations, closure of them will have very little effect on good customers who are rail connected.

This brings us to question (c) on page 37 'To what extent could expenses be saved if some or all of the traffic were not carried?'.

The main elements in direct expenses, which vary in relative importance according to the circumstances of particular traffics, are:—

> Road collection and delivery.
> Terminal expenses.
> Trip working.
> Marshalling.
> Trunk haulage.
> Provision of wagons.
> Documentation.

It is fairly obvious that most of these expense items could be reduced if the traffic which gives rise to them were discontinued. Nevertheless, it is also clear that the extent of the reductions which could be made would depend upon the degree to which facilities used are shared with other traffics, because big savings are often possible only where facilities can be removed altogether.

This is particularly true of costs of small terminals and of the road operations, the rail pick-up services, and the documentation work associated with them. In large terminals, services and staff can normally be scaled down to match the traffic, so that only certain overhead charges remain unchanged, but such scaling down is not possible with smaller terminals, where the time of individual members of the staff is spread over various forms of traffic, where the number of road vehicles cannot be reduced in proportion to the traffic, and where the frequency of trip working cannot be reduced just because the number of wagons to be handled comes down.

The foregoing considerations suggest that station based traffic as a whole should be treated in the same way as the whole railway problem, and that potentially good parts should be improved and developed while basically bad parts should be rejected. With this in mind, the conclusion has been reached that, although a great deal of the traffic which flows to stations from private sidings may be made profitable, and will be developed, very little of it goes to the enormous number of small stations throughout the country, and, therefore, very little of it will be affected if they are closed. It has also been concluded that most of the traffic which does pass through small stations is of the worst kind, which cannot be made to pay at all, and which the railways would do well to lose. Further, it has been concluded that, if the traffic is got rid of, the expenses associated with the traffic will not be saved effectively unless the stations themselves are closed, and where possible, the route as well. It would serve little purpose to thin out the traffic without closing the stations.

So far, attention has been paid only to existing rail traffic of the mineral and general merchandise types, but studies were also made of the traffic not on rail. Before passing on to consideration of potential traffic, however, let us sum up what is proposed for existing traffic.

		m. tons		m. tons	
I	Siding/Siding Siding/Dock	62·5	By block train	30	Keep and improve operating efficiency
			By wagon forwarding	32·5	Keep, but increase through-train working. Some of small siding traffic to Liner Train
II	Siding/Station	12·8	Keep as much as can be handled in a remunerative way. The high proportion which moves in dense inter-city flows is good Liner Train traffic		
	Siding/Road	5·8			
III	Other station traffics	7·9	Attract to Liner Trains that portion which moves in the dense inter-city flows, but shed the rest by station closures and rate increases		
	TOTAL ..	89			

In group II, 64 per cent. of the traffic moves over 75 miles and 50 per cent. of it moves more than 100 miles. In group III, the corresponding figures are 66 per cent. and 50 per cent. Nearly all of the traffic in group II loads well and is of a physical nature which makes it suitable for Liner Train movement. Also most of it will move over the dense inter-city routes. Therefore, at least half of the total 18·6 m. tons, i.e. nearly all which goes over 100 miles, and a part of that which moves over 75 miles, may be regarded highly suitable for Liner Train movement. (Say 10 m. tons.)

The traffics which make up group III are largely composed of smaller consignments than group II and they include a great deal of poor loading traffic. In general, therefore, they are less well suited to Liner Train movement than those in group II. Moreover, a lesser proportion of the total movement of these traffics will be in the dense inter-city flows which the Liner Train is intended to deal with. Probably, therefore, not more than about 2 m. tons of this kind of existing rail traffic will be attracted to Liner Trains in future.

The Survey of Traffic Not On Rail

It is commonly stated that the railways now carry only about a fifth of the freight traffic of the country other than coal, but this figure is based upon a global assessment of the ton-mileage of road vehicles. Taken at its face value, it suggests that there is a large volume of traffic which could be attracted to rail, by suitable services at the right prices. Before such a conclusion can safely be drawn, however, it is necessary to know much more about the nature of this traffic in terms of all the characteristics which determine its relative suitability for road and rail transport. Among other things, it is necessary to know:—

    The nature of the commodity;
    Loadability;
    Points of origin;
    Terminal conditions;
    Volume and regularity of flow;
    Average consignment size;
    Geographical location of flows;
    Lengths of haul;
    How carried at present.

To get this information, a very massive enquiry was made during 1961. The way in which it was carried out is described in Appendix 1, which also gives a summary of the results which it produced.

The enquiry covered 305 m. tons of freight other than coal, of which the railways carried 82 m., and it is estimated that this was over 80 per cent. of the total freight movement in the country, apart from local delivery services by light vehicles.

All of the flows making up the total 223 m. tons of non-railborne traffic were examined to determine their potential suitability for rail haulage. As a result, 130 m. tons had to be judged unsuitable on first inspection, mainly because the length of haul was too small, but also because of terminal considerations, irregularity of flow, requirements for special vehicles, etc. Table 23 of Appendix 1 shows that 62 m. tons of the total travels less than 25 miles, and a further 54 m. tons travels less than 50 miles. Such short distance traffic is unlikely to be attracted to rail unless it can be moved in bulk, directly between rail connected terminals. A very high proportion of this short distance traffic is made up of road stone or building materials moving to contractors' sites, petrol being delivered to service stations, farm produce moving to markets, or fertilizer moving to farms, and other flows to places where no rail terminal could be expected to exist.

The 93 m. tons of traffic which was left after this first sieving was judged potentially suitable for rail haulage by virtue of its physical characteristics and the distance over which it moved. It represents a very large part of the total longer distance road freight of the country, and the way in which it flows is illustrated diagrammatically in Map No. 5.

Features which are strikingly illustrated by the map, although not in themselves surprising, are the concentration of flows between areas of high industrial and population density, paralleling the better used rail routes, and the sparsity of traffic in the green-field areas where rail traffic is also very light. This holds promise for the future profitability of the main rail network, because of the prospect of loading routes more nearly to capacity, but provides no support for continued operation of lightly loaded parts of the system.

After the map had been prepared, the flows composing the 93 m. tons of longer distance traffic was screened again in more detail. By then, progress with other studies had made it clear that traffic could not truly be regarded as potentially good rail traffic for the future unless it could be made to pass as siding traffic, or else could be carried over distances of not less than 70 to 100 miles by Liner Trains. The second examination was, therefore, made with these two possibilities in mind. This showed that there are flows amounting to 13 m. tons which could pass siding to siding, in consignments of substantial size, of which 8 m. tons is suitable for through train movement. It also showed streams of traffic, amounting to a total of 16 m. tons, which were judged to be good Liner Train traffics.

Efforts are already being made to attract to rail the potential siding/siding traffic revealed by the survey, particularly that which can be moved by block trains. Nevertheless, much more vigorous selling is called for, and it will be more soundly based as movement by wagon forwarding is subjugated to through train traffic.

Where desired, and where justified by the volume and regularity of traffic flow, trains of wagons tailored to the special requirements of customers will be operated as timetabled trains.

Liner Trains

Although sundry references have been made to Liner Trains in earlier sections, the nature of this form of service has not, so far, been described.

The Liner Train concept is described more fully in Appendix 4. It has not yet been developed quite to the point where proposals for the establishment of a national network of Liner Train services can be put forward as a firm project, sufficiently detailed to justify capital expenditure, but enough scheme work has been done to show its promise. More thorough market research is going on now, side by side with route selection, studies of depot design and location, and more reliable costing.

The basic idea is to combine road and rail movement in such a way as to take advantage of the low cost of fast through-train movement as the means of providing trunk haulage over medium to long distances, for flows of traffic which, though dense, are composed of consignments too small in themselves to justify through-train operation, and to do so without the disadvantages of either costly assembly of trains by wagon-load movement on rail, or costly transfer of merchandise between road and rail vehicles.

The method proposed for doing this is to link main centres of industry and population by services of fast, regularly scheduled, through-running trains. These trains would be composed of specially designed, permanently coupled, low, flat wagons capable of taking large containers of the newly recommended international cross section of 8 ft. by 8 ft. with length modules of 10, 20 and 30 ft. They would operate in shuttle services between main centres, or over circuits linking a number of centres, and would remain continuously coupled as trains. Containers, loaded at the point of origin of the freight, would be brought to special depots feeding the services by flat-decked road vehicles, or by pickup on rail where conditions made that favourable, and would then be transferred to the Liner Train. At the receiving depot, the procedure would be reversed.

A key to the success of this type of operation is quick safe transfer of containers from one vehicle to another, and feasibility and cost studies have been made of a number of possible ways of doing it. Several methods are satisfactory, and choice will depend to a large extent upon the levels of traffic which depots and services are expected to handle.

The advantages offered by this form of service are:—

   (i) Fast through working of trains to cheapen the trunk haul.

   (ii) Containers designed for easy loading by forklift trucks through full-width end and side doors.

   (iii) Elimination of the expensive double handling associated with the transfer of non-containerised freight from road to rail, and vice versa.

   (iv) Elimination of expensive wagon movement on rail to assemble freight from small terminals into trains.

   (v) Elimination of marshalling and absence of all shunting shocks.

   (vi) Fast, reliable, scheduled delivery.

(vii) Freedom from pilferage.

(viii) Drastic reduction of documentation.

(ix) A system which is simple and readily understandable.

(x) Door-to-door costs below road costs for distances of about 100 miles and very substantially below for longer hauls.

Attention was drawn in earlier sections to the availability of about 12 m. tons/year of very promising Liner Train freight among the unremunerative freight traffics which at present flow through stations. In addition, there is the prospect of transferring a large part of the passenger parcels traffic to these trains with an opportunity to improve handling. Also, and possibly more important, there is the prospect of transferring to them that part of the sundries traffic which moves between main centres, and which amounts to about 3 m. tons per year.

In addition to the railborne traffic suitable for transfer to this type of service there are, as indicated by the freight survey, about 16 m. tons per year of road-borne traffic which could be moved more cheaply by Liner Trains. There is, therefore, at present traffic levels, a potential market of about 30 m. tons, and this should grow at least as fast as the national economy, and rise to 40 m. tons over the next ten years.

Liner Train routes which are being considered are shown on Map No. 11, and figures giving the potentially suitable traffic flowing each way between the main areas which they link are given in Appendix 4.

At present, it is envisaged that there would be about 55 special terminals to feed and link these services, and the approximate location of these terminals is also indicated on the map.

Appendix 4 also includes a tentative estimate of the capital cost of equipping the network shown on Map No. 11, and of the revenue and costs associated with operating it at three different levels of traffic flow. The results are summarised below:—

Capital Cost

	£m.
Depots	16
Locomotives and wagons	34
Road vehicles	25
Containers	25
TOTAL ..	100

Traffic level 1973 estimate	Direct cost £m.	Revenue £m.	Margin £m.
(A) 6,440 m. ton miles	49	67	18
(B) 3,220 m. ton miles. 50 per cent. of (A) level	30	33	3
(C) 9,660 m. ton miles. 150 per cent. of (A) level	74	101	27

At the level of traffic envisaged it is estimated that the services would contribute £18 m. to system cost, as compared with an estimated deficit on existing traffics of the same kind of £31·8 m.

43

These figures are based upon the assumption that British Railways would provide all the road vehicles and carry out all collection and delivery. This would not be their wish or intention, and it is expected that many customers will prefer to use their own vehicles for the purpose. It is expected, also, that some public road hauliers will wish to use Liner Train services for trunk hauls of traffic collected and delivered by themselves.

Subject to a satisfactory outcome from the studies now in hand, it is expected that proposals for construction of the first two Liner Trains will be put forward in a few weeks, and it will then be possible to have them in operation by the end of 1964. One of them would then be used to run two round trips per day between London and Liverpool, and the other would do one round trip per day linking Sheffield with London and Birmingham.

It is clear, however, that the real issue is much bigger than the question as to whether two prototype trains should be produced and put in service. If the Liner Train type of service is judged to be a likely success on the scale envisaged, and likely to contribute very materially to the future viability of the trunk line network of the railways, then it is clearly desirable to introduce a system of services as quickly as possible. Decision on speedy provision of a system as distinct from isolated services is also important from the point of view of attracting custom, because manufacturers may well be prepared to equip themselves to use a system which will give good national coverage, but be unwilling to do so in order to use only one route.

Therefore, the important decision which will have to be made as quickly as possible is whether an integrated system of Liner Train services, such as that shown by Map No. 11, should be set up. If this decision can be reached in a few months, then it should be possible to build up the pattern of services progressively from the end of 1964, at a rate which would bring the full network proposed into operation by 1970.

Freight Sundries

A country wide service is provided by the railways for freight consigned in quantities too small to be treated as a single wagon load, and most of it is carted by road at both ends of the transit. At one time, the railways were the only providers of this kind of service, but now it is shared with road hauliers who are estimated to carry about 55 per cent. to 60 per cent. of the total. As with other forms of freight, however, the railways are still heavily influenced by their former common carrier obligations and by their tradition of nation wide coverage, while the road operators select good traffics and good areas for coverage.

Traffic of this kind tends to decline because of the changing pattern of production and distribution, and the railways' carryings of sundries has declined over recent years. In 1960, the tonnage carried was 3·6 m. and in 1961–62 it was 3·4 m.

As is indicated by the global cost figures for this class of traffic, on page 8, it failed to cover its direct costs in 1961 by £13·5 m., receipts being £38·0 m. with direct costs of £51·5 m., and an assessed overall loss of £21·3 m.

In 1961 a special study was made of the sundries handling problem. This included a test of all the traffic handled on one day, which, because of the diversity of this traffic and the large number of consignments covered, gave a

44

representative sample. The study also included detailed costing of the traffic, and this not only confirmed the previous global estimates of the deficit but also gave quantitative indications of how large savings could be made by different methods of handling.

By the time of the test, the bulk of the traffic had been concentrated upon 550 stations throughout the country, but a further 400 stations still dealt with some of it. As with other traffics, the disparity in the loading of stations handling this traffic is very pronounced, as shown by Table 27, Appendix 1.

Before considering some other features of this traffic, it is worth devoting a little attention to the way in which, with a given total volume, the problem is intensified by handling it through a large number of terminals. For purposes of illustration it is convenient to consider, say, 1,000 terminals with equal throughput and each equally likely to send traffic to any of the others. Then, if the total traffic is 10,000 tons/day, each terminal will receive 10 tons and each will transmit 0·01 tons to every other terminal. If, on the other hand, the same total tonnage were to be concentrated upon 100 rail heads, each would receive 100 tons, and would transmit 1 ton to each of the others, so that daily consignments between terminals would be 100 times as great.

Although, in practice, terminals are far from equal in size, multiplicity of terminals tends to have this same effect. This is important with wagon-load freight, because it reduces the proportion of the traffic which can be handled by through trains. In just the same way, with sundries traffic it reduces the proportion which can be handled by the through loading of full vans.

Even at the best, sundries are a poor loading form of traffic, but the sub-division of flows by the multiplicity of terminals makes it necessary to dispatch vans part filled, to and from many of the lesser used terminals, or to combine loads to different destinations in one van for part of their journey and then tranship them at points along their route. This transhipment involves expensive handling.

At present, with the existing number of terminals, both these expedients are found necessary. As a consequence, the average wagon load is only 0·92 tons, and, in spite of the fact that there is a proportion of through van movement, consignments are, on average, transhipped more than once per journey.

As a result of the study, it is now proposed to reduce the number of main depots progressively to about 100, to limit light van loading and transhipment by reducing the frequency of forwarding to and from smaller stations in the meanwhile, and to concentrate transhipments on a few strategically placed points. At the same time, charges scales are being adjusted to bring them more into line with costs, and the present expensive documentation procedure is being simplified.

The volume and geographical distribution of present flows are shown by Map No. 7.

Full implementation of the plan, as it stands at present, would lead to a distribution of depots as shown by Map No. 8. It would involve the provision or re-equipment of a number of depots, at an estimated capital cost of £11 m., and, taken together, all the changes proposed under the plan would be expected to reduce costs by £20 m., at the present level of traffic.

While this would be a great improvement on the present deficit of £14 m., it does not make the traffic particularly attractive. Therefore, the plan will be implemented as far as possible without any major capital expenditures, and decisions about new depots will be deferred until the effects of : concentration upon existing depots, modified charging scales, new documentation, and other changes under the plan have been tested.

Another reason for deferring decisions on the provision of new depots is that the ultimate handling and profitability of this traffic is seen to be related to the future of ' Liner Trains ', which, if introduced as a network, will cheapen the rail handling of a large part of the sundries traffic flows and provide through-train movement in place of the present wagon forwarding for much of it. Also, the use of containers, and sub-containers or pallets, will facilitate more efficient handling in the sundries sheds than is possible with existing rail wagons.

Further, since Liner Trains will offer speed and regularity comparable with passenger trains, they will open the way for a combination of the sundries and passenger parcels services, with a corresponding improvement in loadings and in overhead expenses.

Sundries traffic, together with parcels, accounts for the employment of about three-quarters of the road vehicle fleet, which cost £21·88 m. in 1960 and £22·15 m. in 1961. Costs will go on rising unless drastic steps are taken, because of increases in wages and materials and, also, because of the growing size and congestion of urban areas. With this in mind, a General Manager of railway cartage services has been appointed to exercise central control so far as is necessary to achieve efficient and co-ordinated use of the road fleet.

Reduction of the Freight Wagon Fleet

The way in which the freight wagon fleet of the railways has varied over the post-war period is shown in Table 2, Appendix 3. The table below shows capacity, together with the volume of freight carried, and the average ' turn-round time '. The fleet was sharply reduced in 1962, but the railways still had 848,591 wagons at the end of the year as will be seen from the figures which follow:—

Year	Number of wagons at 1st January	Tonnage capacity	Number of wagons forwarded loaded (000's)	Tonnage forwarded (000's)	Average turn-round time (days)
1946 ..	1,252,000	..	39,765	262,400	9·45
1947 ..	1,230,000	..	37,549	257,300	9·83
1948 ..	1,209,380	..	36,431	276,117	9·96
1949 ..	1,165,166	14,560,402	36,220	280,170	9·65
1950 ..	1,098,614	14,004,049	35,750	281,348	9·22
1951 ..	1,089,975	14,134,260	35,496	284,803	9·21
1952 ..	1,094,144	14,401,226	34,978	284,916	9·38
1953 ..	1,105,130	14,743,949	34,760	289,271	9·54
1954 ..	1,107,110	14,957,544	34,246	283,498	9·70
1955 ..	1,109,690	15,264,316	31,990	274,177	10·41
1956 ..	1,109,935	15,555,896	31,598	276,957	10·54
1957 ..	1,102,607	15,731,251	30,822	274,283	10·73
1958 ..	1,090,114	15,846,352	27,063	242,873	12·08
1959 ..	1,005,526	14,981,743	25,750	233,963	11·71
1960 ..	945,260	14,264,830	26,356	248,500	10·76
1961 ..	946,998	14,339,097	24,851	238,177	11·43
1962 ..	941,543	14,347,572	22,580	227,675	12·51
1963 ..	848,591	13,198,121			

The meaning of 'turn-round time' needs to be explained, otherwise it is a misleading expression. It is the average time from loading to reloading for all wagons, derived by dividing the total number of wagon days per year by the total number of wagon loadings per year. Therefore, high turn-round time may well indicate high wagon capacity relative to the availability of traffic rather than slowness of movement. That this is so is fairly evident from the Table. Turn-round time rose from 9·45 days in 1946 to 12·51 days in 1962, but the actual speed of movement of wagons almost certainly increased. Far more striking is the fluctuation between 1957 and 1958. There is no reason to suppose that speed of movement dropped in 1958, but there was a fall in the economy and rail traffic fell by 12 per cent. As a result, turn-round time rose by an exactly similar amount.

Opinion has varied from time to time as to the optimum size of the wagon fleet, but it has now been decided, quite apart from the intolerably high cost of a fleet of the present size, that it is far bigger than it needs to be for the traffic carried with any regularity throughout the year. Figures which support this view are given below:—

NET TON MILES AND LOADED WAGON MILES PER WAGON IN STOCK 1961

	All traffic	Merchandise only	Coal and other minerals only
Net ton miles (000's)	17,590,315	5,533,160	12,031,155
Average number of wagons	944,270	433,438	510,832
Net ton miles per wagon:			
(a) per annum	18,628	12,812	23,564
(b) per week	358	246	453
Average wagon load (tons)	7·9	4·1	13·5
Loaded wagon miles per week	45	60	33

DIVISION OF WAGON AND CONTAINER TURN-ROUND TIME

Type of wagon or container	Number at end 1961	Turn-round time (available stock)	Terminal time	Movement time		Remainder	Remainder expressed as a percentage of movement and terminal time
				Loaded	Empty		
		days	days	days	days	days	
Wagons							
Open goods ..	232,416	13·4	4·5	1·9	0·6	6·4	91·5
Covered goods	140,043	5·8	2·9	1·4	0·4	1·1	23·4
Mineral ..	508,816	10·6	3·7	1·7	1·2	4·0	60·6
Steel carrying	55,279	11·7	4·7	1·9	1·5	3·6	44·4
Others (cattle)	4,989	20·2	2·0	2·0	3·0	13·2	188·6
Containers							
Open	7,309	32·0	6·4	1·6	1·0	23·0	255·5
Covered ..	18,172	10·8	4·3	1·4	0·7	4·4	68·7
Others ..	22,815	13·8	4·1	1·4	1·0	7·3	112·3

47

The next to last column shows the time which is unaccounted for because wagons are standing idle somewhere away from terminals and not in the course of movement. Therefore, this time, expressed as a percentage of the terminal time plus movement time, gives a measure of the gross surplus capacity which exists. Clearly, with a system of the type which we have, and with seasonal fluctuations in load, some surplus is necessary, but surpluses as large as some of those indicated by the figures are clearly excessive.

Other relevant factors are: the changing pattern of traffic, the movement towards more through-train working, the elimination of the poor wagon utilisation at small stations and on branch lines, and the obsolescence of much of the stock. All these reinforce the view that rapid reduction of the fleet should continue. The position will be reviewed as reduction proceeds, but it is expected that at least 348,000 wagons will be scrapped over the next 3 years, with a total annual saving of £10 m.–£12 m. per annum thereafter.

The reductions which were made in 1962, and the position as it will be at the end of 1963, and those planned for 1963 are shown below. The condemnations already decided upon for 1963 can be seen from the following summary, and further withdrawals in the year may yet be decided upon.

SUMMARY OF STOCK POSITION OF
WAGONS AND CONTAINERS, 1961–1962–1963

Wagons

Type	Stock at 31st December, 1961	Stock at 31st December, 1962	Anticipated stock at 31st December, 1963	Reduction in 1963 compared with 1961
Open	232,416	191,563	152,466	79,950
Covered	140,043	136,199	134,086	5,957
Mineral	508,816	464,199	416,607	92,209
Cattle	4,989	4,409	2,500	2,489
Steel carrying ..	55,279	52,221	42,899	12,380
TOTAL ..	941,543	848,591	748,558	192,985

Containers

Type	Stock at 31st December, 1961	Stock at 31st December, 1962	Anticipated Stock at 31st December, 1963	Reduction in 1963 compared with 1961
Open	7,309	6,782	1,763	5,546
Covered	18,172	17,389	14,200	3,972
Others	22,815	22,364	20,348	2,467
TOTAL ..	48,296	46,535	36,311	11,985

OPERATING AND ADMINISTRATIVE ECONOMIES

So far, attention has been devoted to the consideration of changes in the broad pattern of the Railways' activities, but the large scope for economies by improving the way in which things are done is not being neglected. It is impossible to describe all the steps which are being taken, but since it is not very convincing merely to mention the matter without giving any details, some of the more important and interesting activities are touched upon below.

Railway costs are, to a predominant degree, incurred on a time basis, over 60 per cent. of the total is the cost of manpower, and the greater part of the remainder is the cost of providing equipment. Costs which are the equivalent of raw material cost in a manufacturing industry are comparatively small. There are, therefore, real opportunities for cost savings by improving the effectiveness with which men and machines are employed. For example, great scope for economy lies in the improvement of utilisation of locomotives, wagons, containers, coaches, cartage vehicles and the staff associated with their use and maintenance.

An important element is maintenance. Maintenance practices are being subjected to much closer control, and, helped by the reduction in the steam locomotive fleet and the elimination of the older types of wagon and coach, the annual burden is already being very considerably reduced.

The workshops are being rationalised and, apart from the fall in the work load which is already taking place and which may be accelerated, this will result in a reduction of £4 m. in standing charges by 1966.

There is considerable scope for the introduction of mechanical handling equipment to deal more efficiently with existing traffics. The assistance of expert consultants in this field has been enlisted to study methods of handling and carrying parcels and freight sundries. Worthwhile improvement, leading to increased efficiency and greater reliability of service, is expected.

Progress is being made in rationalising the multiplicity of specifications for equipment, materials and stores. This should lead to cost reductions on components manufactured in the workshops and price benefits on purchases from suppliers. A saving of only 1 per cent. on purchase prices for materials would represent £1 m. per annum. Reduction in stocks of stores is being actively pursued and, during 1962, the capital tied up in this way was reduced by £15 m.

In 1961, operation of the railway-owned road vehicle fleet cost £22 m. Study of existing operating practices, standardisation, and improved maintenance techniques should reduce the fleet and improve operations and service. In this field also, the help of experienced operators has been sought. Already it has become apparent that any extra cartage arising out of line and station closures can be undertaken without any addition to the total fleet and staff.

In 1957 an agreement was made in regard to manning of diesel and electric locomotives and multiple units. The contribution made by the Unions was of considerable value. The rapid development of the new forms of traction makes it desirable to seek agreement to further progress in the field of train manning, and discussions are taking place.

Maintenance of signalling equipment, production and repair of wagon sheets, creosoting of timber, quarrying, and concrete component manufacture, are all examples of widely diverse activities associated with the railway, which are being subjected to study and thought.

49

Documentation imposes a heavy burden upon almost every form of railway activity and it is a field in which considerable economies can be found by simplifying procedures.

At centres where large numbers of men are employed it is always possible to improve productivity. One adverse factor of importance is partitioning of duties and multiplicity of staff grades. This is a field in which big improvements can be made, with Union help.

Because of the nature of the business, the efficiency of the railways is influenced by the decisions of a large number of people in charge of widely dispersed local operations, from District Officers down to station masters, yard masters, and others. The arrangements to ensure that all these people become better acquainted with the costs of the operations which they control are being steadily improved with encouraging results.

Savings are also expected in the interest burden, and in bank charges, through the tight control of credit, the better use of funds, and the rationalisation of banking services.

Work study techniques have been applied to a variety of railway activities, but most extensively to permanent way maintenance. In collaboration with the Unions, efforts are constantly being made to extend these techniques over a wider field of work.

REDUCTION IN MANPOWER

The changes proposed in foregoing parts of the Report are expected to lead to very substantial economies and, since staff cost is such a high proportion of total cost, this inevitably means that there must be associated reductions in the number of people employed. The Board is very conscious of the human problems which this will cause, but, as will be seen from what follows, the necessary reductions can be achieved by some acceleration of a process which is already in train, rather than by creation of redundancy upon a completely new scale.

The number of staff employed on the railway in all grades at 29th December 1962, was 474,538, broadly divided as follows:—

Grade	Number
Administrative, technical and clerical	71,933
Station masters, supervisors and control staff ..	22,488
Traffic wages staff	223,346
Maintenance and construction	145,399
Miscellaneous	11,372
	474,538

and the way in which staff has been reduced over a period of years is shown by the following table:—

Year	Number of staff	Cumulative reduction on 1948	
		No.	per cent.
1948	648,740		
1953	593,768	54,972	8·5
1958	550,123	98,617	15·2
1959	518,863	129,877	20·0
1960	514,500	134,240	20·7
1961	500,434	148,306	22·9
1962	474,538	174,202	26·9

Annual reductions have been continuous, and that for 1962 was 25,896, but it has been possible to bring them about with less widespread disturbance than might be supposed because there is a high natural wastage of staff, and a total replacement rate of around 80,000 per year.

The extent to which the rate of reduction will be accelerated cannot be forecast with accuracy, because most of the changes will be of a continuing nature with no precisely foreseeable end point, and because the rate at which some changes can be made will depend upon external factors which are not under the control of the railways.

The effect of the closures of services, lines and stations which are firmly proposed can be assessed fairly closely, and is rather less than might be expected. This position arises because there has long been an awareness of the poverty of these parts of the system, and staff has already been brought down as far as possible, consistent with safety and the pattern of service still being given.

As a consequence, closures of lightly used parts of the system cause staff reductions which are far from proportional to the number of stations or the route mileage affected.

The distribution of 73,551 staff of one of the larger Regions, between stations, depots, yards and all other points of employment, is shown in the following table:—

TABLE SHOWING STAFF DISTRIBUTION BY STATIONS AND DEPOTS

Range	Stations and depots		Staff		Cumulative figures			
	Number	Percentage of total	Number	Percentage of total	Stations and depots	Per cent	Staff	Per cent
Up to 5	251	30·0	762	1·0				
6–10	147	17·6	1,162	1·6	398	47·6	1,924	2·6
11–20	195	23·3	2,926	4·0	593	70·9	4,850	6·6
21–50	118	14·1	3,650	5·0	711	85·0	8,500	11·6
51–100	40	4·8	2,771	3·7	751	89·8	11,271	15·3
101–200	32	3·9	4,540	6·2	783	93·7	15,811	21·5
201–300	13	1·5	3,270	4·4	796	95·2	19,081	25·9
301–500	12	1·4	4,810	6·6	808	96·6	23.891	32·5
501–1,000	15	1·8	10,249	13·9	823	98·4	34,140	46·4
1,001–2,000	7	0·9	10,920	14·9	830	99·3	45,060	61·3
2,001–3,000	1	0·1	2,641	3·6	831	99·4	47,701	64·9
3,001–4,000	1	0·1	3,946	5·3	832	99·5	51,647	70·2
4,001–5,000	2	0·25	8,444	11·5	834	99·8	60,091	81·7
Over 5,000	2	0·25	13,460	18·3	836	100·0	73,551	100·0

The best estimate that can be made of the number of staff whose services will no longer be required in connection with the operation of the passenger services listed in Appendix 2 is 16,200. They are, of course, spread over the country, and the number includes those affected by closures which were already in the process of being dealt with in August 1962, and which were suspended until this plan appeared.

51

Subsequent complete closure of lines, after arrangements have been made to retain any good rail freight which they carry, will add to the number of staff displaced. A first assessment of the effect of the more obvious cases puts the number at 10,900 but, as in the case of the passenger services, reshaping will be a continuous process and further reductions will follow.

Like other changes, introduction of the freight sundries plan will be a progressive process, but when it is fully developed, it will lead to a direct reduction in supervisory, clerical and handling staff, which is estimated to be 8,600, to which must be added a longer term saving of train working and maintenance staff estimated to be 4,900.

Reductions in coaching and wagon stock, and in locomotives, may make it necessary to re-examine the workshop position, once implementation of the plan is well under way, although reductions of the order of those proposed were taken into account in the recently prepared Workshop Plan.

Indirect savings in administrative staff will accrue when reductions in services have a group effect. In addition, the wholesale re-diagramming of locomotives, multiple units, coaches and trainmen, which will be made possible when a certain stage of withdrawal has been reached, will lead to better utilisation of what remains. Determination of the future position of alternative main routes, and large termini serving the same places, will result in further savings.

The manpower reductions likely to result from all these changes cannot yet be established. However, preliminary examination in some areas leads to the conclusion that the figures given for direct savings from line closures will be no more than one half of those which will ultimately be achieved.

For the financial well-being of the railways, it is necessary that changes be made as quickly as possible, but there will be many retarding factors.

Hitherto, station closures, withdrawals of passenger services and curtailments of freight facilities, have been pursued at a rate which was very largely governed by the management's capacity to investigate, document and present a succession of individual cases to both Transport Users Consultative Committees and Staff representatives. As a consequence, it has taken 12 years to withdraw unprofitable passenger or freight services from 4,236 route miles.

Effective implementation of the plan will depend upon a speedier realisation of intentions than has been found possible in the past. Even so, a staff displacement will clearly be a continuing process over a number of years, and the average rate of reduction need not be very much higher than the 1962 rate. There may, however, if the consultative procedure operates with reasonable speed, be an initial period when the closure of the passenger services and of some lines will release staff at a higher rate than the expected average. In part, this will be due to the holding back of cases which were in the pipeline last August.

Fortunately the extent to which men will have to be discharged will be far lower than the annual reductions in manpower. Natural wastage is such that the major part of the reductions can be brought about by strict control of recruitment, and this control will be facilitated by the existence of a clear cut plan. Even so, because the pattern of staff displacement will not match the pattern of wastage, problems will also arise from the necessity for extensive re-deployment of people.

The Board is keenly aware that a large scale reorganisation of the kind outlined in this Report is bound to cause hardship to some people and inconvenience to many others, and has prepared to ameliorate these difficulties as far as possible.

The established arrangements for redundancy have been revised and men who have to move from their appointed post to another one in a lower grade will in future retain their old rate of pay for up to five years, unless they can be reinstated in their former grade in the meantime. If they have to move home, there are substantial payments to meet their removal costs.

For those who have to be discharged, either because there is no other work which they can go to, or who elect to leave rather than move to other work, there will be adequate periods of notice during which they will be able to travel free and with pay to seek other employment. Also, there will be substantial resettlement payments.

The scheme for resettlement payments, which has recently been agreed with the Railway Trade Unions, provides for lump sum payments which depend upon length of service, plus continuing weekly payments over a period related both to length of service and age. The continuing payments are designed to help men while they are seeking other employment. For some long service men, lump sums may amount to nearly £500, and weekly payments to supplement unemployment pay may continue for a year.

In addition, of course, efforts will be made to help men to find new employment, by using existing machinery for placement and re-training, and by consultation with other employers.

On the positive side, the Board hopes that formulation of a realistic plan will restore confidence in the future of the railways and remove the anxiety which has existed in the minds of many for some years. A vigorous and efficient railway system, of the right size and pattern, will be able to offer good employment and wide opportunities for promotion to the large number of staff who will remain, and to those who will come in future.

THE FINANCIAL CONSEQUENCES OF THE PLAN

A summary, in broad terms, of the improvements in the working results of British Railways which it is estimated will result from the measures and proposals described in the plan is given below. Some of the savings would be more direct, immediate, and calculable, than others, but where ranges are shown they give a rough indication of the measure of uncertainty.

To a large degree, proposals included in the plan are interdependent. Condensation of the system, elimination of uneconomic services and traffics, reduction in rolling stock, through-train working at the expense of wagon forwarding, the build-up of traffic on the main route network, and reduction of administrative expenses, are all closely linked. Therefore, realisation of many of the savings depends upon adoption of the plan as a whole. If the plan is implemented with vigour, however, much (though not necessarily all) of the Railways' deficit should be eliminated by 1970.

It is also important to realise that the elimination of cost factors will exceed the net savings expected from the various changes, and this will reduce the vulnerability of the Railways to further cost increases. At present, increases in the costs associated with the large volume of hopelessly unremunerative activities progressively undermine the potentially good railway services.

	Estimated financial improvement of the order of £ m. per annum	
Discontinuance and rationalisation of stopping passenger services and closure of stations to passenger traffic (after allowing for loss of contributory revenue) ..	18	
Subsequent closure of lines and reduction from passenger to freight standard of maintenance of other lines following the withdrawal of services and closure of stations	11–13	
Discontinuance of local freight services and closure of stations to freight traffic (after allowing for the preservation of potentially good traffics by alternative arrangements)	5–10	
Direct savings arising from closures		34–41
Reduction in the fleet of gangwayed passenger coaches by the withdrawal of the stock reserved for peak traffics (after allowing for some loss of earnings)	2–3	
Reduction in the fleet of wagons	10–12	
Rationalisation of workshops—reduction in standing charges (apart from the effect of the fall in work load)	4	
Continued conversion of steam to diesel traction.. ..	15–20	
Reduction in the expenses of working coal traffic by— (a) the establishment of coal concentration depots in collaboration with the National Coal Board and the distributors, and (b) increased movement of coal in block train loads following the provision of train loading facilities at collieries	7–10	

	Estimated financial improvement of the order of £ m. per annum
Concentration of sundries traffic	15–20
Introduction and development of Liner Trains—net earnings in five years time, say	10–12
Reduction in the loss on existing unprofitable traffics by commercial measures, say, ...	5–6
Additional net earnings assuming that traffic not on rail but which on several screenings, including cost screening, is seen to be favourable to rail, is secured to the extent of half the potential volume in the next five years, say, ...	10–15
Reduction in the expenses of general administration ..	3–4

These estimates are not fully additive but are not subject to any serious measure of overlap.

The list is not an exhaustive summary of the measures referred to in the body of the Report. In particular, whilst some of the estimates reflect improvements in efficiency associated with major changes, no figure is included to cover the summation of a multiplicity of efficiency improvements of a more detailed kind, which could be made with or without the plan. At this time, and in the face of great change, it would be unrealistic to formulate such an estimate, but there can be no doubt that higher standards of utilisation of staff and equipment will bring substantial rewards.

The proposals in respect of the continued replacement of steam by diesel traction, the introduction of Liner Trains, and the reorganisation of the arrangements for Sundries traffic, would involve capital expenditure of the order of £250 m. There would, therefore, be a substantial rise in interest charges to set against the estimated financial improvement credited to these proposals.

In addition to the proposals referred to in the plan, major modernisation works are already in hand, including the electrification on the London Midland Region. These modernisation works will themselves contribute to the improvement in the financial position of British Railways.

OTHER FACTORS INFLUENCING THE FUTURE ROLE OF THE RAILWAYS

The proposals put forward in this Report have been formulated for the purpose of shaping the railways towards a sound and viable condition in the future, without assuming any major changes in the role which they are expected to fill or in the framework within which they are expected to operate. The Railways Board is aware, however, that direct measurement of profitability is not the only criterion which can be applied when determining the best use of railways as a part of the transport system, in relation to the social and industrial structure as a whole. The Board is satisfied, however, that, although they have not shaped their proposals upon the basis of hypothetical changes beyond their control, or with regard to responsibilities which do not at present rest upon them, none of the proposals put forward here does violence to concepts which others might reasonably have wished to include.

Factors which need mentioning in this connection are:—

(i) Rationalisation of transport as a whole.

(ii) Total social benefit, as distinct from immediate profit.

(iii) Long-term trends in location of industry and population.

(iv) Prevention of industrial growth by withdrawal of railway services.

Rationalisation of Transport as a Whole

Consideration of the best use of national resources will lead most people to the conclusion that some co-ordination of the various modes of transport is necessary. This view is bound to present itself very forcefully to those responsible for railways, which are especially vulnerable to uncontrolled development of transport capacity, because of their high fixed investment and their correspondingly high break-even level of traffic. Nevertheless, sound co-ordination must be based upon the use of each form of transport for those purposes for which it is the best available means, and, as has already been emphasised, all the changes proposed are directed towards making the railways best in fields where they clearly have the potential to be so, and towards withdrawing them from fields in which they are clearly not the best means of meeting the need. Between these two fields in which the case is black and white, there is a wide field over which the balances between road and rail, or rail and air, might be critically influenced by future changes in circumstances or legislation. But none of the present proposals penetrates into this field to the point of prejudicing future judgments.

Any deliberate influencing of the balance between different forms of transport, in future, is more likely to be in favour of the railways than against them. This would improve the financial position of the densely loaded main lines, and increase the proportion of intermediately loaded routes which could be made viable in future, but it could not, within the bounds of reason, be carried so far as to justify the network of lightly loaded routes which are to be closed.

Total Social Benefit

It might pay to run railways at a loss in order to prevent the incidence of an even greater cost which would arise elsewhere if the railways were closed. Such other costs may be deemed to arise from congestion, provision of parking space, injury and death, additional road building, or a number of other causes.

It is not thought that any of the firm proposals put forward in this Report would be altered by the introduction of new factors for the purpose of judging overall social benefit. Only in the case of suburban services around some of the larger cities is there clear likelihood that a purely commercial decision within the existing framework of judgment would conflict with a decision based upon total social benefit. Therefore, in those instances, no firm proposals have been made but attention has been drawn to the necessity for study and decision.

Long-Term Trends in the Location of Industry and Population

No novel assumptions have been made about the future distribution of population and industry in the country as a whole. Implicitly, it has been assumed that the pattern will continue to be basically similar to that which exists at present and that, while there may be a continuation or a reversal of existing trends, there is not likely to be any change so radical as to affect the desirability of building up as much as possible of the main line network of services, or of withdrawing rural services which are lightly used both because of low population density and because of the growth of alternative means of transport.

The trend towards concentration of industry and population in the South-East is unfavourable to the future of the main line network of the railways and it would be beneficial if it were reversed. Failure to suppose any reversal of the trend has not, however, led to any proposal to modify main line routes.

The building of a Channel Tunnel will also have a favourable effect on the railways, unless it greatly intensifies migration to the South-East, but, here again, the benefit will be to the main line traffics and, perhaps in particular, to Liner Train types of service. Nothing prejudicial to future rail developments in connection with a Channel link is proposed, and Liner Train services will be planned with the Tunnel in mind.

Prevention of Industrial Growth by Withdrawal of Railway Services

The point has been made in the previous section that there is no proposal to weaken the main line network within the country, so that there will be no inhibition of a general re-location of industry and population as a result of the proposals put forward. It can be argued, however, that re-location on a smaller scale may be affected by closure of lightly used branches and extensions of the main routes.

This may conceivably be true, but it must be recognised that most of the lines to be closed have already been in existence for some fifty to a hundred years, and their existence has not induced development so far. Indeed, in most cases the trend has been in the opposite direction. Therefore, in formulating proposals for line closure, all the Railway Regions have taken account of any developments which are sufficiently specific to be probable, but have not been influenced by quite unsupported suggestions that something might happen some day.

SUMMARY OF THE REPORT

The Report describes the investigations carried out, the conclusions which were drawn, and the proposals which are made for the purpose of reshaping British Railways to suit modern conditions.

The thought underlying the whole Report is that the railways should be used to meet that part of the total transport requirement of the country for which they offer the best available means, and that they should cease to do things for which they are ill suited. To this end, studies were made to determine the extent to which the present pattern of the railways' services is consistent with the characteristics which distinguish railways as a mode of transport, namely:—the high cost of their specialised and exclusive route system, and their low cost per unit moved if traffic is carried in dense flows of well-loaded through trains. As a result, it is concluded that, in many respects, they are being used in ways which emphasise their disadvantages and fail to exploit their advantages.

The proposals for reshaping the railways are all directed towards giving them a route system, a pattern of traffics, and a mode of operation, such as to make the field which they cover one in which their merits predominate and in which they can be competitive.

To this end, it is proposed to build up traffic on the well-loaded routes, to foster those traffics which lend themselves to movement in well-loaded through trains, and to develop the new services necessary for that purpose. At the same time, it is proposed to close down routes which are so lightly loaded as to have no chance of paying their way, and to discontinue services which cannot be provided economically by rail. These proposals are, however, not so sweeping as to attempt to bring the railways to a final pattern in one stage, with the associated risks of abandoning too much or, alternatively, of spending wastefully.

Although railways can only be economic if routes carry dense traffic, density is so low over much of the system that revenue derived from the movement of passengers and freight over more than half the route miles of British Railways is insufficient to cover the cost of the route alone. In other words, revenue does not pay for the maintenance of the track and the maintenance and operation of the signalling system, quite apart from the cost of running trains, depots, yards and stations. Also, it is found that the cost of more than half of the stations is greater than the receipts from traffic which they originate.

Amongst traffics, stopping passenger services are exceptionally poor. As a group, they are very lightly loaded and do not cover their own movement costs. They account for most of the train miles on much of the lightly loaded route mileage, but also account for a considerable train mileage on more heavily loaded routes, and are one of the main causes for the continued existence of many of the small and uneconomic stations.

Fast and semi-fast, inter-city passenger trains are potentially profitable and need to be developed selectively, along with other forms of traffic on trunk routes. High peak traffics at holiday periods are, however, very unremunerative. They are dying away and provision for them will be reduced.

Suburban services feeding London come close to covering their full expenses, but give no margin to provide for costly increases in capacity, even though they are overloaded and demand goes on increasing.

Suburban services feeding other centres of population are serious loss makers, and it will not be possible to continue them satisfactorily without treating them as a part of a concerted system of transport for the cities which they serve.

Freight traffic, like passenger traffic, includes good flows, but also includes much which is unsuitable, or which is unsuitably handled by the railways at present. The greater part of all freight traffic is handled by the staging forward of individual wagons from yard to yard, instead of by through-train movement. This is costly, and causes transit times to be slow and variable. It also leads to low utilisation of wagons and necessitates the provision of a very large and costly wagon fleet.

Coal traffic as a whole just about pays its way, but, in spite of its suitability for through train movement, about two thirds of the total coal handled on rail still moves by the wagon-load. This is very largely due to the absence of facilities for train loading at the pits, and to the multiplicity of small receiving terminals to which coal is consigned. Block train movement is increasing, but substantial savings will result from acceleration of the change. This depends, in turn, upon provision of bunkers for train loading at the pits, bunkers for ship loading at the ports, and of coal concentration depots to which coal can be moved by rail for final road distribution to small industrial and domestic consumers.

Wagon-load freight traffic, other than coal, is a bad loss maker when taken as a group, but over half of it is siding-to-siding traffic, much of which moves in trainload quantities, and this makes a good contribution to system cost. One third of the remainder moves between sidings and docks, and this falls just short of covering its direct costs. The remaining 30 per cent. of the whole passes through stations, at one or both ends of its transit, and causes a loss relative to direct expenses which is so large that it submerges the credit margin on all the rest.

Freight sundries traffic is also a bad loss maker. It is handled at present between over 900 stations and depots, which causes very poor wagon loading and a high level of costly transhipment of the freight while in transit. Railways handle only about 45 per cent. of this traffic in the country, and do not select the flows which are most suitable for rail movement. If they are to stay in the business, British Railways must concentrate more upon the inter-city flows and reduce the number of depots handling this form of traffic to not more than a hundred.

Study of traffic not on rail shows that there is a considerable tonnage which is potentially good rail traffic. This includes about 8 m. tons which could be carried in train-load quantities, and a further 30 m. tons which is favourable to rail by virtue of the consignment sizes, lengths of haul, and terminal conditions. In addition, there is a further 16 m. tons which is potentially good traffic for a new kind of service—a Liner Train service—for the combined road and rail movement of containerised merchandise.

Preliminary studies of a system of liner train services, which might carry at least the 16 m. tons of new traffic referred to above and a similar quantity drawn from traffic which is now carried unremuneratively on rail, show such services to be very promising and likely to contribute substantially to support of the main railway network, if developed.

The steps proposed, to achieve the improvements referred to above, are:—

(1) Discontinuance of many stopping passenger services.
(2) Transfer of the modern multiple unit stock displaced to continuing services which are still steam locomotive hauled.
(3) Closure of a high proportion of the total number of small stations to passenger traffic.
(4) Selective improvement of inter-city passenger services and rationalisation of routes.
(5) Damping down of seasonal peaks of passenger traffic and withdrawal of corridor coaching stock held for the purpose of covering them at present.
(6) Co-ordination of suburban train and bus services and charges, in collaboration with municipal authorities, with the alternative of fare increases and possible closure of services.

(7) Co-ordination of passenger parcels services with the Post Office.

(8) Increase of block train movement of coal, by:—
   (a) inducing the National Coal Board to provide train loading facilities at collieries;
   (b) inducing the establishment of coal concentration depots, in collaboration with the National Coal Board and the distributors.

(9) Reduction of the uneconomic freight traffic passing through small stations by closing them progressively, but with regard to the preservation of potentially good railway traffics, and by adjustment to charges.

(10) Attraction of more siding-to-siding traffics suitable for through-train movement by operating such trains at the expense of the wagon forwarding system and by provision of time-tabled trains, of special stock, to meet customer requirements.

(11) Study and development of a network of 'Liner Train' services to carry flows of traffic which, though dense, are composed of consignments too small in themselves to justify through-train operation.

(12) Concentration of freight sundries traffic upon about 100 main depots, many of them associated with Liner Train depots, and carriage of main flows of sundries on Liner Trains, probably coupled with passenger parcels, and possibly Post Office parcels and letters.

(13) Rapid, progressive withdrawal of freight wagons over the next three years.

(14) Continued replacement of steam by diesel locomotives for main line traction, up to a probable requirement of at least 3,750/4,250 (1,698 already in service and 950 on order at present).

(15) Rationalisation of the composition and use of the Railways' road cartage fleet.

These various lines of action are strongly interdependent. If the whole plan is implemented with vigour, however, much (though not necessarily all) of the Railways' deficit should be eliminated by 1970.

TRAFFIC STUDIES

61

TRAFFIC STUDIES

In July 1961 a number of traffic studies were embarked upon designed to obtain much more information than had hitherto been available regarding the working of the railway and its future prospects. These embraced the following:—

(1) A study to determine the contribution each station, depot, and section of line makes to the system as a whole in both the passenger and freight fields.

(2) A cost study to establish the characteristics of all wagon-load freight traffic and to determine which traffics were profitable to the railway and under what conditions.

(3) A study to ascertain the pattern and characteristics of all wagon-load mineral and merchandise traffic not passing by rail and the volume, direction, distance, and terminal requirements of that part of it judged to be favourable to rail. The study included consideration of how the traffic would be carried by rail.

(4) A study, similar to No. (3), in respect of coal class traffic.

(5) A study to establish the volume and characteristics of less than wagon-load traffic with the object of deciding upon the practicability of devising a plan for remunerative handling of this type of traffic.

Whilst each of the Studies yielded information which was of value in itself, the group of Studies was planned so that results could be integrated for the purpose of determining the shape and size of a railway fitted to present day conditions and requirements.

The outcome of these studies is described in considerable detail in the pages which follow and is illustrated by tables, graphs and maps.

LINE DENSITY OF PASSENGER AND FREIGHT TRAFFIC

In 1961 the route mileage open to traffic was 17,830. The density of passenger and freight traffic over each section of route, excluding certain areas of considerable complexity, was assessed during a normal week.

The following tables show the disparity between the different parts of the system measured by the percentage of passenger miles and freight ton miles occupying the route mileage in the groups.

Table No. 1

DENSITY OF PASSENGER TRAFFIC

Range—passenger miles	Route miles		Percentage of total passenger miles
	Actual	Percentage of total	
	(Figures in brackets are cumulative)		
Less than 2,000 passenger miles ..	6,056	36	1
2,000–9,999	4,612	27 (63)	7 (8)
10,000–19,999	2,186	13 (76)	10 (18)
20,000–39,999	1,982	11 (87)	17 (35)
40,000–79,999	1,349	8 (95)	23 (58)
80,000–179,999	689	4 (99)	24 (82)
180,000 passenger miles and over ..	188	1 (100)	18 (100)
TOTAL	17,062	100	100

DENSITY OF FREIGHT TRAFFIC

Range—ton miles	Route miles		Percentage of ton miles
	Actual	Percentage of total	
	(Figures in brackets are cumulative)		
Less than 5,000 ton miles	7,221	42	3
5,000–19,999 tons	4,061	24 (66)	13 (16)
20,000–39,999 tons	2,648	16 (82)	21 (37)
40,000–69,999 tons	1,779	10 (92)	25 (62)
70,000–99,999 tons	949	6 (98)	22 (84)
100,000 ton miles and over	404	2 (100)	16 (100)
TOTAL	17,062	100	100

DENSITY OF PASSENGER AND FREIGHT TRAFFIC

Range— passenger miles combined with ton miles	Route miles		Percentage of passenger/ton miles
	Actual	Percentage of total	
	(Figures in brackets are cumulative)		
Less than 10,000	6,633	39	3
10,000–39,999	4,690	28 (67)	16 (19)
40,000–79,999	2,890	17 (84)	23 (42)
80,000–119,999	1,586	9 (93)	23 (65)
120,000–249,999	1,067	6 (99)	25 (90)
250,000 units and over	196	1 (100)	10 (100)
TOTAL	17,062	100	100

63

The distribution of traffic between the least used and most used parts of the system is also illustrated by Figure No. 1.

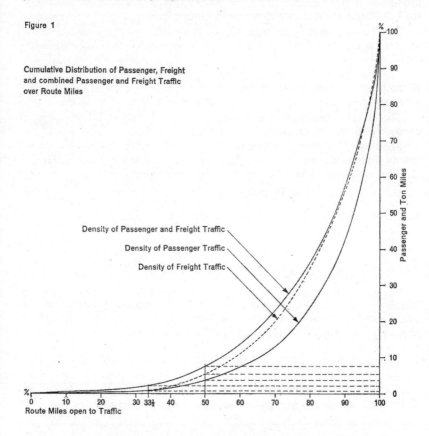

Figure 1

Cumulative Distribution of Passenger, Freight and combined Passenger and Freight Traffic over Route Miles

Density of Passenger and Freight Traffic

Density of Passenger Traffic

Density of Freight Traffic

Passenger and Ton Miles

Route Miles open to Traffic

It will be seen that one-third of the route mileage carries only 1 per cent. of the total passenger miles. Similarly, one-third of the mileage carries only 1 per cent. of the total freight ton miles, and the corresponding figures for the least used half are 4 per cent. and 5 per cent. of passengers and freight respectively. It will also be seen that one-third of the route mileage carries only $2\frac{1}{2}$ per cent. of the total passenger and freight traffic, combined by adding passenger miles and ton miles as equal units, and half the route mileage carries only $7\frac{1}{2}$ per cent. of the total traffic.

Maps Nos. 1 and 2 show the distribution of passenger and freight traffic density over the railway route system. The volume passing in a normal week is indicated either by broken lines of different types or by continuous lines indicating density by their thickness.

There is a striking disparity between the heavily loaded and extremely lightly loaded lines shown on the maps.

It is noticeable, from both maps, that the majority of the little-used lines are away from main centres of population, industrial areas, centres of raw material production, and the major ports. As would be expected, the main routes between the key centres are those which are most used.

The two most striking differences between the map showing passenger travel and the map showing freight traffic occur in London and in the Leeds–Sheffield–Derby area.

The dominance of London in the passenger field as compared with the rest of the country is well illustrated. Equally, the freight movement in the industrial area mentioned dominates the freight picture.

The heavier passenger travel outside London and the large cities is concentrated on a lesser number of routes than is freight.

Short distance passenger movement into and out of the major cities is clearly seen. Much of this is twice daily peak travel at sub-standard fares, and the line thicknesses should be interpreted with this in mind.

Line densities are not the only measure of the use made of the railway and in the sections which follow the contribution made by stations in the fields of passenger travel and freight movement are given in supporting tables. Any apparent discrepancies in totals are due to rounding.

DISTRIBUTION OF PASSENGER TRAFFIC—STATION RECEIPTS

There are marked disparities in the contribution which stations make to passenger traffic. Whilst passenger receipts are not necessarily a true measure of the contribution each station makes, because some receive more traffic than they originate, they can be regarded as a reasonable guide.

Passengers

An analysis of the revenue accruing from passengers during 1960 at 4,300 stations which were still open to passengers at the end of 1962 is given in the following table:—

Table No. 4

PASSENGER RECEIPTS

(*per annum*)

Range of passenger receipts	Number of stations		Passenger receipts	
	Actual	Percentage of total	£'000	Percentage of total
		(Figures in brackets are cumulative)		
Less than £2,500	1,762	41	1,429	1
£2,500–£9,999	1,119	26 (67)	6,028	5 (6)
£10,000–£49,999 ..	884	21 (88)	20,220	16 (22)
£50,000–£199,999 ..	406	9 (97)	39,484	30 (52)
£200,000–£499,999 ..	95	2 (99)	28,226	22 (74)
£500,000 and over	34	1 (100)	34,196	26 (100)
TOTAL	4,300	100	129,584	100

It will be seen, from Figure No. 2 which follows, that one third of the stations contributed only 1 per cent. to passenger revenue, and that half of the total number contributed only 2 per cent.

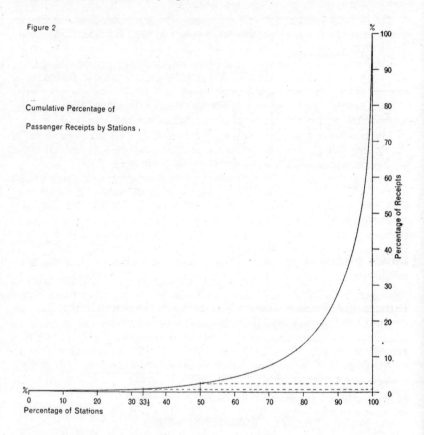

Figure 2

Cumulative Percentage of Passenger Receipts by Stations

The geographical distribution of the stations throughout the country, together with an indication of the contribution each makes to passenger revenue, is shown in Map No. 3. It will be seen that the smaller stations are not necessarily confined to areas and lines of low density, although, as would be expected, it is in such localities that they predominate.

Parcels Traffic

Most passenger stations also deal with railway parcels and miscellaneous traffic by coaching trains although all stations open for parcels do not deal with passengers.

In the following table this traffic arising at the same stations is grouped according to originating receipts.

PARCELS RECEIPTS

(*per annum*)

Range of receipts	Number of stations		Parcels receipts	
	Actual	Percentage of total	£'000	Percentage of total
(Figures in brackets are cumulative)				
Less than £500	2,457	57	341	1
£500–£2,499	911	21 (78)	1,179	3 (4)
£2,500–£9,999	531	12 (90)	2,896	8 (12)
£10,000–£49,999 ..	301	7 (97)	7,025	19 (31)
£50,000–£299,999 ..	78	2 (99)	8,863	24 (55)
£300,000 and over ..	22	1 (100)	16,352	45 (100)
TOTAL	4,300	100	36,656	100

The disparity between stations is again seen. Naturally most of the parcels traffic originates in, and is destined for, areas of dense population. It is not, therefore, surprising that at one end of the scale 2,457 or 57 per cent. of the stations, contribute only 1 per cent. of the parcels receipts, whilst at the other end 100 stations or 3 per cent. account for 69 per cent. of the receipts.

DISTRIBUTION OF FREIGHT TRAFFIC—STATION TONNAGE AND RECEIPTS

Most stations, particularly the smaller ones, deal with freight traffic in addition to passenger and parcels traffic. The respective levels of utilisation are not necessarily the same for passengers, parcels and freight traffics at individual stations, but in general they are similar.

Tables showing the 1960 tonnage of forwarded and received merchandise and minerals, and received coal traffic at 5,031 stations which were open at the end of 1962, follow:—

Table No. 6

MERCHANDISE AND MINERALS FORWARDED

(*per annum*)

Volume of traffic (tons)	Number of stations		Tonnage	
	Actual	Percentage of total	'000 tons	Percentage of total
(Figures in brackets are cumulative)				
Less than 500 tons ..	2,906	58	243	1
500–2,499	1,124	22 (80)	1,389	8 (9)
2,500–9,999	668	13 (93)	3,395	20 (29)
10,000–49,999	276	6 (99)	5,685	33 (62)
50,000 tons and over ..	57	1 (100)	6,513	38 (100)
TOTAL	5,031	100	17,225	100

MERCHANDISE AND MINERALS RECEIVED

(per annum)

Volume of traffic (tons)		Number of stations		Tonnage	
		Actual	Percentage of total	'000 tons	Percentage of total
		(Figures in brackets are cumulative)			
Less than 500 tons	..	2,526	50	310	1
500– 2,499 ..	..	1,175	24 (74)	1,413	5 (6)
2,500–9,999 ..	..	762	15 (89)	3,887	15 (21)
10,000–49,999 ..	..	453	9 (98)	9,354	35 (56)
50,000 tons and over	..	115	2 (100)	11,726	44 (100)
TOTAL ..	..	5,031	100	26,690	100

COAL CLASS TRAFFIC RECEIVED

(per annum)

Volume of traffic (tons)		Number of stations		Tonnage		Number of wagons	
		Actual	Percentage of total	'000 tons	Percentage of total	'000 wagons	Percentage of total
		(Figures in brackets are cumulative)					
Nil	..	1,172	23	0	..	0	..
1–999 tons	..	1,007	20 (43)	395	1 (1)	39	2 (2)
1,000–2,499 ..	..	783	16 (59)	1,326	5 (6)	123	5 (7)
2,500–4,999 ..	..	653	13 (72)	2,364	8 (14)	211	9 (16)
5,000–24,999 ..	..	1,181	24 (96)	12,619	45 (59)	1,121	45 (61)
25,000–49,999 ..	..	171	3 (99)	5,840	21 (80)	510	21 (82)
50,000 tons and over ..		64	1 (100)	5,513	20 (100)	459	18 (100)
TOTAL ..	..	5,031	100	28,057	100	2,463	100

A feature is that, although the tonnage of coal received by the smaller stations is small, it is greater than the combined forwarded and received tonnage of minerals and merchandise.

The table which follows shows the position when the forwarded and received traffic is aggregated.

TOTAL FREIGHT TRAFFIC

(*per annum*)

Volume of traffic (tons)	Number of stations		Tonnage	
	Actual	Percentage of total	'000 tons	Percentage of total
	(Figures in brackets are cumulative)			
Less than 2,500 tons ..	1,938	38	3,057	4
2,500–9,999	1,592	32 (70)	8,505	12 (16)
10,000–24,999	833	17 (87)	13,200	18 (34)
25,000–99,999	554	11 (98)	26,110	36 (70)
100,000 tons and over ..	114	2 (100)	21,781	30 (100)
TOTAL	5,031	100	72,653	100

The geographical distribution of the stations throughout the country, together with an indication of the tonnage passing through each, is shown in Map. No. 4.

On Page 11 of the Report there is a reference to the revenue derived from freight traffic at the least used stations. Table No. 10 and Figure No. 3 show the originating receipts at the 5,031 stations during 1960.

FREIGHT TRAFFIC RECEIPTS

(*per annum*)

Size groups (originating freight receipts) £'s	Number of stations		Receipts	
	Actual	Percentage of total	£'000	Percentage of total
	(Figures in brackets are cumulative)			
Less than 1,500	2,906	58	2,104	3
1,500–9,999	1,324	26 (84)	5,818	10 (13)
10,000–49,999	468	9 (93)	10,685	18 (31)
50,000–199,999	276	6 (99)	21,357	34 (65)
200,000 and over ..	57	1 (100)	21,710	35 (100)
TOTAL	5,031	100	61,674	100

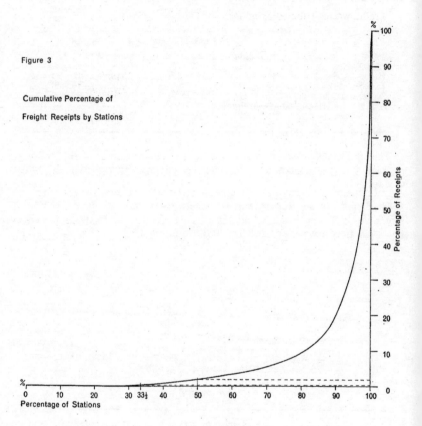

Figure 3

Cumulative Percentage of

Freight Receipts by Stations

Percentage of Receipts

Percentage of Stations

During the survey of freight traffic in April 1961, the opportunity was taken to record the volume of freight traffic dealt with at the stations which forwarded and received full wagon loads during that week. The results are of some interest compared with the very much more extensive record represented by Tables Nos. 6 to 9 of this Appendix. They are also a pointer to the extent to which many stations deal with no full load traffic at all, for quite considerable periods.

Traffic was distributed as under:—

STATIONS
(*Excluding Private Sidings*)

			Tons ('000)	Number of stations
Minerals and merchandise				
Forwarded	..	..	190	2,067
Received	..	..	370	2,990
Coal class				
Received	..	..	372	3,124

In all, 4,371 stations were concerned in the despatch and receipt of 932,000 tons of traffic.

STATIONS
(*Including Private Sidings*)

			Tons ('000)	Number of stations
Minerals and merchandise				
Forwarded	..	..	1,695	2,871
Received	..	..	1,695	3,749
Coal class				
Received	..	..	2,737	3,590

In all, 4,995 stations and associated private sidings were concerned in the despatch and receipt of 4·4 m. tons of traffic.

Even after making allowance for the fact that the record covered only one week, and for seasonal variations, a striking feature of the analysis was the number of stations which dealt with no freight traffic. There is no doubt that all stations play some part at some period of the year, but it is reasonable to assume that a large proportion of them only receive and forward traffic intermittently.

The eight tables which follow show the participation, firstly, of stations alone and, secondly, of stations including the private sidings associated with them.

MINERAL AND MERCHANDISE TRAFFIC FORWARDED FROM STATIONS
(EXCLUDING PRIVATE SIDINGS)

Week ended 23rd April, 1961

Volume of traffic (tons)	Number of stations		Volume of traffic	
	Number	Percentage of total	'000 tons	Percentage of total
	(Figures in brackets are cumulative)			
Less than 10 tons ..	602	29	2·5	1
10–19	322	16 (45)	4·5	2 (3)
20–49	451	22 (67)	14·8	8 (11)
50–99	264	13 (80)	19·3	10 (21)
100–199	192	9 (89)	27·9	15 (36)
200–499	168	8 (97)	53·4	28 (64)
500–999	50	2 (99)	35·3	19 (83)
1,000–1,999	14	1 (100)	18·9	10 (93)
2,000 tons and over ..	4	.. (100)	13·6	7 (100)
TOTAL	2,067	100	190·3	100

MINERAL AND MERCHANDISE TRAFFIC RECEIVED AT STATIONS
(EXCLUDING PRIVATE SIDINGS)

Week ended 23rd April, 1961

Volume of traffic (tons)	Number of stations		Volume of traffic	
	Number	Percentage of total	'000 tons	Percentage of total
	(Figures in brackets are cumulative)			
Less than 10 tons ..	876	29	3·7	1
10–19	466	16 (45)	6·3	2 (3)
20–49	591	20 (65)	19·0	5 (8)
50–99	342	11 (76)	25·2	7 (15)
100–199	282	9 (85)	41·3	11 (26)
200–499	265	9 (94)	86·7	23 (49)
500–999	110	4 (98)	80·2	22 (71)
1,000–1,999	40	1 (99)	53·3	14 (85)
2,000 tons and over ..	18	1 (100)	54·3	15 (100)
TOTAL	2,990	100	370·0	100

COAL CLASS TRAFFIC RECEIVED AT STATIONS
(EXCLUDING PRIVATE SIDINGS)

Week ended 23rd April, 1961

Volume of traffic (tons)	Number of stations		Volume of traffic	
	Number	Percentage of total	'000 tons	Percentage of total
	(Figures in brackets are cumulative)			
Less than 10 tons ..	101	3	0·8	..
10–19	607	19 (22)	7·8	2 (2)
20–49	859	28 (50)	27·3	7 (9)
50–99	580	19 (69)	41·1	11 (20)
100–199	486	16 (85)	67·7	18 (38)
200–499	353	11 (96)	103·6	28 (66)
500–999	107	3 (99)	71·6	19 (85)
1,000–1,999	24	1 (100)	28·5	8 (93)
2,000 tons and over ..	7	.. (100)	23·2	7 (100)
TOTAL	3,124	100	371·6	100

MINERAL AND MERCHANDISE FORWARDED AND RECEIVED AND COAL CLASS TRAFFIC RECEIVED—STATIONS
(EXCLUDING PRIVATE SIDINGS)

Week ended 23rd April, 1961

Volume of traffic (tons)	Number of stations		Volume of traffic	
	Number	Percentage of total	'000 tons	Percentage of total
	(Figures in brackets are cumulative)			
Less than 10 tons ..	458	10	2·1	..
10–19	557	13 (23)	7·5	1 (1)
20–49	917	21 (44)	30·3	3 (4)
50–99	701	16 (60)	50·2	5 (9)
100–199	633	14 (74)	91·4	10 (19)
200–499	640	15 (89)	204·5	22 (41)
500–999	268	6 (95)	190·8	20 (61)
1,000–1,999	148	4 (99)	200·4	22 (83)
2,000 tons and over ..	49	1 (100)	154·5	17 (100)
TOTAL	4,371	100	931·9	100

When private siding traffic is included, as shown in the following tables, it is noticeable that the effect at the lower levels is negligible. It will be seen from the above table that 1,932 stations, 44 per cent. of the total, dealt with only

40,000 tons, or 4 per cent. of the total at all stations. In Table No. 18, 2,356 stations with their associated private sidings, 48 per cent. of the total, dealt with 84,300 tons or 2 per cent. of the total of 4·4 m. tons passing during the test period.

Table No. 15

MINERAL AND MERCHANDISE TRAFFIC FORWARDED FROM STATIONS AND PRIVATE SIDINGS

Week ended 23rd April, 1961

Volume of traffic (tons)	Number of stations		Volume of traffic	
	Number	Percentage of total	'000 tons	Percentage of total
	(Figures in brackets are cumulative)			
Less than 20 tons ..	938	33	7·4	..
20–49	493	18 (51)	16·2	1 (1)
50–99	347	12 (63)	25·5	2 (3)
100–199	297	10 (73)	43·7	3 (6)
200–499	321	11 (84)	104·8	6 (12)
500–999	178	6 (90)	126·3	7 (19)
1,000–1,999	126	4 (94)	182·1	11 (30)
2,000–4,999	99	3 (97)	319·7	19 (49)
5,000–9,999	44	2 (99)	306·2	18 (67)
10,000–19,999	20	1 (100)	323·7	19 (86)
20,000 tons and over ..	8	.. (100)	239·8	14 (100)
TOTAL	2,871	100	1,695·4	100

Table No. 16

MINERAL AND MERCHANDISE TRAFFIC RECEIVED AT STATIONS AND PRIVATE SIDINGS

Week ended 23rd April, 1961

Volume of traffic (tons)	Number of stations		Volume of traffic	
	Number	Percentage cf total	'000 tons	Percentage of total
	(Figures in brackets are cumulative)			
Less than 20 tons ..	1,294	34	10·2	..
20–49	669	18 (52)	22·0	1 (1)
50–99	446	12 (64)	32·6	2 (3)
100–199	379	10 (74)	55·0	3 (6)
200–499	434	12 (86)	141·6	8 (14)
500–999	240	6 (92)	172·8	10 (24)
1,000–1,999	144	4 (96)	205·8	12 (36)
2,000–4,999	80	2 (98)	251·4	15 (51)
5,000–9,999	39	1 (99)	282·6	17 (68)
10,000–19,999	14	1 (100)	188·7	11 (79)
20,000 tons and over ..	10	.. (100)	332·8	21 (100)
TOTAL	3,749	100	1,695·4	100

COAL CLASS TRAFFIC RECEIVED AT STATIONS AND PRIVATE SIDINGS

Week ended 23rd *April*, 1961

Volume of traffic (tons)	Number of stations		Volume of traffic	
	Number	Percentage of total	'000 tons	Percentage of total
	(Figures in brackets are cumulative)			
Less than 20 tons ..	694	19	8·5	..
20–49	814	23 (42)	26·5	1 (1)
50–99	559	16 (58)	40·3	1 (2)
100–199	498	14 (72)	71·0	3 (5)
200–499	431	12 (84)	130·3	5 (10)
500–999	214	6 (90)	151·6	6 (16)
1,000–1,999	130	4 (94)	178·6	7 (23)
2,000–4,999	134	4 (98)	420·0	15 (38)
5,000–9,999	57	1 (99)	403·5	15 (53)
10,000–19,999	41	1 (100)	559·3	20 (73)
20,000 tons and over ..	18	..	747·6	27 (100)
TOTAL	3,590	100	2,737·2	100

MINERALS AND MERCHANDISE FORWARDED AND RECEIVED AND COAL CLASS TRAFFIC RECEIVED—STATIONS AND PRIVATE SIDINGS

Week ended 23rd *April*, 1961

Volume of traffic (tons)	Number of stations		Volume of traffic	
	Number	Percentage of total	'000 tons	Percentage of total traffic forwarded*
	(Figures in brackets are cumulative)			
Less than 20 tons ..	884	18	8·7	..
20–49	796	16 (34)	26·5	1
50–99	676	14 (48)	49·1	1
100–199	661	14 (62)	95·8	2
200–499	702	14 (76)	228·8	5
500–999	415	8 (84)	299·6	7
1,000–1,999	319	6 (90)	458·1	10
2,000–4,999	302	6 (96)	941·1	21
5,000–9,999	122	2 (98)	858·6	19
10,000–19,999	73	1 (99)	1,056·5	24
20,000 tons and over ..	45	1 (100)	2,105·5	47
TOTAL	4,995	100		

* The total volume of traffic forwarded was 4·4 m. tons.

DISTRIBUTION OF FREIGHT TRAFFIC—PRIVATE SIDINGS

A considerable proportion of the freight carried by rail is dealt with through private sidings and, as in the case of stations, there is a large number through which very little traffic passes.

The tables which follow show the number of loaded wagons forwarded and received during 1960.

Table No. 19

PRIVATE SIDING TRAFFIC FORWARDED
(*per annum*)

Number of wagons	Number of private sidings		Wagons	
	Actual	Percentage of total	'000 wagons	Percentage of total
	(Figures in brackets are cumulative)			
Less than 50 wagons ..	2,559	43	16	0
50–499	1,245	21 (64)	251	1 (1)
500–2,499	944	16 (80)	1,118	6 (7)
2,500–9,999	624	11 (91)	3,570	20 (27)
10,000–29,999	392	7 (98)	6,814	38 (65)
30,000 wagons and over..	130	2 (100)	6,441	35 (100)
TOTAL	5,894	100	18,210	100

It will be seen that 3,804 sidings forwarded only 1 per cent. of the traffic, whereas at the other end of the scale, 130 sidings accounted for 35 per cent.

Table No. 20

PRIVATE SIDING TRAFFIC RECEIVED
(*per annum*)

Number of wagons	Number of private sidings		Wagons	
	Actual	Percentage of total	'000 wagons	Percentage of total
	(Figures in brackets are cumulative)			
Less than 50 wagons ..	2,011	34	18	0
50–499	1,782	30 (64)	373	3 (3)
500–2,499	1,216	21 (85)	1,366	10 (13)
2,500–9,999	601	10 (95)	3,322	23 (36)
10,000–29,999	189	3 (98)	3,056	22 (58)
30,000 wagons and over..	95	2 (100)	5,891	42 (100)
TOTAL	5,894	100	14,026	100

The pattern is similar to the forwarded position, 3,793 sidings receiving only 3 per cent. of the wagons, whilst 95 sidings received 42 per cent.

PRIVATE SIDING TRAFFIC FORWARDED AND RECEIVED

(*per annum*)

Number of wagons	Number of private sidings		Wagons	
	Actual	Percentage of total	'000 wagons	Percentage of total
	(Figures in brackets are cumulative)			
Less than 50 wagons ..	1,033	17	16	0
50–499	1,642	28 (45)	359	1 (1)
500–2,499	1,464	25 (70)	1,774	6 (7)
2,500–9,999	900	15 (85)	4,781	15 (22)
10,000–29,999	621	11 (96)	10,687	33 (55)
30,000 wagons and over..	234	4 (100)	14,619	45 (100)
TOTAL	5,894	100	32,236	100

Clearly, a study of the position of each private siding in the smaller sized groups may well reveal that their usefulness is far removed from what was originally intended.

GENERAL MERCHANDISE AND MINERALS WAGON-LOAD TRAFFICS

During the week ended 23rd April, 1961, a special study was made of wagon-load freight traffic despatched by rail.

The test covered virtually the whole of the traffic forwarded to and from stations and private sidings during the selected week. In relation to the total traffic for 1961, it was estimated to represent about one week's proportion.

The week selected for the test was reasonably representative of the general pattern of the wagon-load traffic carried, although it was appreciated that there were substantial seasonal traffics and that there could be appreciable fluctuations in regular traffics.

The volume of wagon-load General Merchandise and Minerals traffic recorded in the test week was:—

Consignments	..	..	..	..	82,000
Tonnage ..	..	..	..	..	1,695,000
Loaded wagons and containers ..		..	..	182,400
Loaded wagon miles	..	..	..	..	18,652,000

The receipts and estimated costs shown below were:—

Receipts	..	..	..	..	£2,253,000
Estimated direct costs	..	..	..	£2,274,100

77

F

Nature and Characteristics of Traffic Analysed

The tables on pages 82 to 89 together present a comprehensive picture of the wagon-load General Merchandise and Minerals traffic as a whole:—

Tables I, II and III, analyse the traffic in three alternative ways—by terminal conditions, by wagon loading and by transit distance—showing for each grouping the consignments, tonnage, wagons and containers used, direct costs and receipts.

Tables IV, V and VI, give a more detailed analysis of the tonnage and relative profitability of the traffics carried according to the different combinations of terminal conditions, wagon loading and distance.

Terminal Conditions

Table I is an analysis of traffic by various combinations of terminal conditions. The importance of any one of the individual terminal conditions is more strikingly illustrated if the figures are summarised in another way.

The following summary shows the volume of traffic affected by each of the different terminal conditions. Traffic for which the terminal conditions at the forwarding and receiving points are not identical appears under each of the two headings concerned:—

	Tons	Percentage of total traffic
Traffic dealt with by road at one or both ends of the transit	181,300	11
Traffic originating and/or terminating at station	324,000	19
Traffic originating and/or terminating at docks	316,700	19
Traffic originating and/or terminating at private sidings	1,560,400	92

The predominant influence of private sidings suggests that they are a prime factor in the retention to rail of wagon-load merchandise and minerals traffic; only 8 per cent. of the traffic which passed during the test week was not dealt with through a private siding at one end or the other.

Wagon Loading

Table II analyses wagon loading. Whilst 84 per cent. of the total tonnage passes in loads of over 8 tons, there is a substantial amount of traffic which has a very low loading. Some 33,700 consignments, or 41 per cent. of the total, and 50,700 of the wagons forwarded, or 28 per cent. of the total, had loadings of 4 tons or less.

Distance

Table III gives an analysis by distance, whilst an analysis of the average wagon loading according to terminal conditions and distance is shown in Table IV. The relationship between wagon loading and distance shows no consistent pattern, although wagon loading is clearly linked with terminal conditions in that:—

(a) Low wagon loading is generally found when road conveyance features at one end of the transit. For road/road and road/station transits, the average wagon loads over all distances are only 2·2 and 3·1 tons respectively.

(b) Where private siding is one of the terminal conditions this is generally associated with high average wagon loading.

Terminal Conditions and Distance

The pattern of traffic by transit distance, in conjunction with terminal conditions, can also be seen from Table IV. Almost three-quarters of the tonnage falls into the siding/dock and siding/siding combinations of terminal conditions. Over one-half of the siding/dock traffic passes over distances of 25 miles or less, whilst about one-third of the siding/siding traffic is in the same range. Thereafter there is a fairly even spread of siding/siding traffic up to 200 miles. For other combinations of terminal conditions there is some concentration of traffic between 51 and 200 miles; the general pattern is summarised below in Table No. 22:—

Table No. 22

ANALYSIS OF TERMINAL CONDITIONS BY DISTANCE

Transit distance (miles)	Siding/Siding	Dock/Siding	Other terminal conditions	Total
	'000 tons			
1–25	292·1	174·0	48·3	514·3
26–50	200·5	38·9	62·5	301·9
51–100	207·9	23·6	135·4	366·9
101–200	188·0	15·5	166·0	369·5
201–300	46·9	3·3	55·1	105·3
301 and over	10·6	0·9	26·0	37·5
TOTAL	946·0	256·3	493·1	1,695·4

Distance and Wagon Loading

Table VI shows the distribution of traffic by distance and wagon loading, without regard to terminal conditions, in terms of number of wagons. Taking all distances, the number of wagons employed carrying loads of 2 tons and under is almost as great as the number of wagons carrying loads of 12–16 tons. Yet the tonnages conveyed are in the ratio of 1 : 13, viz.:—

	Wagons	Tons
Wagon loading		
Up to 2 tons	25,400	29,900
Over 12 and up to 16 tons	29,900	400,500

79

In total, 28 per cent. of the wagons forwarded during the week carried some 6 per cent. of the traffic in loads of up to 4 tons, the balance of the traffic being carried with an average wagon load of over 12 tons.

Pattern of Relative Profitability

Whilst Tables I, II and III show the receipts, direct costs, and margin on the traffic as a whole, analysed in turn by terminal conditions, wagon loading and distance, these figures tend to obscure the range of results which emerges when the figures are further analysed by combinations of the three factors. The general pattern of profitability of the test week's traffic, as operated at the present time, can be more clearly seen from Tables IV, V and VI.

The tables show the volume of traffic for each heading, the overall margin, + or —, of receipts compared with direct costs, and also in brackets alongside each figure of margin, the percentage ratio of receipts to direct costs.

In all tables which show traffic analysed according to terminal conditions, the headings are arranged in descending order of terminal cost, commencing with road/road—normally the most expensive conditions—and ending with siding/siding at lowest end of the scale. The tables show clearly the gradual trend of improvement in results as the three factors at work—terminal conditions, wagon loading and distance—become more favourable.

Table IV, which analyses the traffic and the results by terminal conditions and distances, shows that the only group of traffic making a contribution above direct costs is that where private sidings are involved at both ends.

At the other extreme, traffic which is dealt with by road at both ends of the transit fails, by a substantial margin, to cover its direct costs. This is primarily attributable to high terminal costs in conjunction with poor wagon loading.

A broadly similar pattern is found for other combinations of terminal conditions where road conveyance is involved.

Table VI shows the results analysed by terminal conditions and wagon loading. The groups of traffic conveyed in wagon loads of up to 6 tons failed to cover direct costs, whatever the terminal conditions. Traffic loaded between 6 and 12 tons per wagon produced little or no margin, except where sidings were used at both ends.

Conclusions

This particular Survey and series of analyses relates to the wagon-load general merchandise and minerals traffic taken as a whole and does not reveal the characteristics and relative profitability of particular commodities or flows of traffic, some of which may show individual patterns materially different. Moreover, it does not follow that all consignments of traffic within a particular group shown in the analyses conform to the overall results disclosed. Nevertheless, a number of facts emerge fairly clearly, and certain broad conclusions can be drawn. They are:—

(1) Traffic involving the higher cost terminal facilities (e.g. road conveyance or station) produces poor wagon loading and usually fails to cover its direct costs.

(2) Traffic involving the lower cost terminal facilities (i.e. private sidings) passes in higher wagon loadings and usually shows some margin over direct costs, except when in combination with one of the unfavourable terminal conditions at the other end of the transit.

(3) Transit distance does not materially alter the general position stated although results are better at the longer distances.

(4) The volume of wagon-load merchandise and minerals traffic which remains on rail and passes under the high terminal cost conditions is relatively very small.

(5) Charges do not adequately reflect the effects of poor wagon loading, high cost terminal conditions, and inflation of costs by declining traffic.

Some more detailed conclusions relating to particular groups are given in the Report.

(87549)

FREIGHT TRAFFIC TEST—GENERAL MERCHANDISE

The following three tables analyse the total traffic according to (a) terminal conditions,

TABLE I—ANALYSIS BY

Combination of terminal conditions (irrespective of the order in which they occur)	Consignments		Tons	
	No.	Per cent.	No.	Per cent.
Road–Road	9,500	11	26,800	2
Road–Station	4,100	5	17,600	1
Road–Dock	2,600	3	25,400	1
Road–Siding	14,000	17	111,500	7
Station–Station	3,800	5	30,200	2
Station–Dock	2,700	3	29,600	2
Dock–Dock	100	..	5,400	..
Station–Siding	16,000	20	246,600	14
Siding–Dock	4,100	5	256,300	15
Siding–Siding	25,100	31	946,000	56
TOTAL	82,000	100	1,695,400	100

TABLE II—ANALYSIS

WAGON-LOAD GROUP (Average wagon or container load per consignment)				
Up to and including 2 tons	19,500	24	29,900	2
Over 2 tons up to and including 4 tons	14,200	17	72,800	4
Over 4 tons up to and including 6 tons	10,100	12	90,000	5
Over 6 tons up to and including 8 tons	6,800	8	91,000	5
Over 8 tons up to and including 12 tons	18,000	22	410,200	24
Over 12 tons up to and including 16 tons	8,700	11	400,500	24
Over 16 tons up to and including 25 tons	4,000	5	474,200	28
Over 25 tons	600	1	126,900	8
TOTAL	82,000	100	1,695,400	100

TABLE III—ANALYSIS

DISTANCE GROUP Miles (chargeable)				
1–25	12,600	15	514,300	30
26–50	9,600	12	301,900	18
51–75	9,000	11	186,300	11
76–100	8,300	10	180,600	11
101–150	14,400	18	220,600	13
151–200	12,300	15	148,900	9
201–300	10,800	13	105,300	6
301 and over	5,000	6	37,500	2
TOTAL	82,000	100	1,695,400	100

Note.—All figures have been rounded to the nearest hundred;

recorded in the week April 17th–23rd (inclusive), 1961,
(b) wagon loading and (c) distance.

TERMINAL CONDITIONS

Loaded wagons and/or containers		Direct costs		Receipts		Margin
No.	Per cent.	£	Per cent.	£	Per cent.	£
12,100	7	214,100	9	145,300	7	— 68,800
5,700	3	91,700	4	64,400	3	— 27,300
5,600	3	91,900	4	61,600	3	— 30,300
21,100	12	376,000	17	299,900	13	— 76,100
5,500	3	91,800	4	66,300	3	— 25,500
5,700	3	72,500	3	65,000	3	— 7,500
1,200	1	9,500	..	3,900	..	5,600
28,100	15	379,600	17	369,500	16	— 10,100
22,500	12	200,900	9	190,500	8	— 10,400
74,800	41	746,200	33	986,500	44	240,300
182,400	100	2,274,100	100	2,252,900	100	— 21,200

BY WAGON LOADING

No.	Per cent.	£	Per cent.	£	Per cent.	£
25,400	14	346,000	15	207,500	9	—138,500
25,300	14	319,600	14	249,800	11	— 69,800
18,900	10	252,400	11	203,900	9	— 48,500
13,800	8	183,800	8	170,800	8	— 13,000
41,900	23	542,800	24	547,100	24	4,300
29,900	16	324,700	14	402,400	18	77,700
23,500	13	261,700	12	386,500	17	124,800
3,700	2	43,000	2	84,800	4	41,800
182,400	100	2,274,100	100	2,252,900	100	— 21,200

BY DISTANCE

No.	Per cent.	£	Per cent.	£	Per cent.	£
43,000	24	301,000	13	210,100	9	— 90,900
26,600	15	237,100	10	249,300	11	12,200
19,800	11	218,300	10	214,900	10	— 3,400
19,200	10	237,300	11	252,100	11	14,800
27,100	15	394,100	17	413,700	18	19,600
21,900	12	359,700	16	370,300	17	10,600
17,300	9	339,500	15	353,600	16	14,100
7,400	4	187,100	8	188,900	8	1,900
182,400	100	2,274,100	100	2,252,900	100	— 21,200

apparent discrepancies in totals and margins are due to this.

83

TABLE IV—ANALYSIS BY TERMINAL

Distance group miles (chargeable)	Road/Road	Road/Station	Road/Dock	Road/Siding
				T O
1–25	700	800	2,100	4,300
26–50	1,900	2,100	4,400	10,000
51–75	1,900	1,400	4,000	11,600
76–100	2,500	2,500	5,400	16,000
101–150	5,300	3,500	4,200	26,100
151–200	5,200	3,100	2,500	20,300
201–300	4,600	2,300	2,400	18,200
301 and over	4,700	1,900	600	5,000
TOTAL	26,800	17,600	25,400	111,500

MARGIN
(the figures in parenthesis show the receipts

Distance group miles (chargeable)	Road/Road	Road/Station	Road/Dock	Road/Siding
1–25	− 2,200 (46)	− 2,000 (45)	− 3,100 (40)	− 4,800 (48)
26–50	− 4,900 (53)	− 3,200 (60)	− 5,500 (51)	− 8,500 (65)
51–75	− 5,700 (54)	− 2,300 (63)	− 6,900 (53)	−10,200 (68)
76–100	− 6,000 (62)	− 2,800 (69)	− 5,800 (65)	−10,200 (75)
101–150	−13,100 (66)	− 5,500 (67)	− 5,400 (69)	−15,400 (80)
151–200	−13,400 (69)	− 4,500 (74)	− 1,900 (83)	−15,900 (80)
201–300	−13,700 (68)	− 5,200 (70)	− 1,300 (89)	− 9,500 (88)
301 and over	− 9,700 (79)	− 1,900 (86)	− 200 (93)	− 1,500 (95)
TOTAL	−68,800 (68)	−27,300 (70)	−30,300 (67)	−76,100 (80)

AVERAGE WAGON

Distance group miles (chargeable)	Road/Road	Road/Station	Road/Dock	Road/Siding
1–25	2·1	2·7	5·9	5·8
26–50	2·4	3·2	4·8	5·3
51–75	2·2	2·8	4·2	5·1
76–100	2·3	4·0	5·4	6·4
101–150	2·1	3·1	4·0	5·9
151–200	2·0	3·0	4·0	4·6
201–300	2·1	2·5	3·9	5·0
301 and over	2·6	3·5	4·2	4·1
TOTAL	2·2	3·1	4·5	5·3

Note.—All figures have been rounded to the nearest hundred;

CONDITIONS AND DISTANCE

Station/Station	Station or Dock/Dock	Station/Siding	Siding/Dock	Siding/Siding	Total
N S					
2,000	8,500	29,900	174,000	292,100	514,300
2,600	2,700	38,900	38,900	200,500	301,900
2,800	7,300	33,800	8,900	114,700	186,300
6,700	5,900	33,800	14,700	93,200	180,600
4,500	4,300	53,200	10,800	108,700	220,600
3,700	2,700	27,300	4,700	79,300	148,900
3,600	3,200	20,700	3,300	46,900	105,300
4,300	500	9,000	900	10,600	37,500
30,200	35,000	246,600	256,300	946,000	1,695,400

—£
expressed as a percentage of direct costs)

Station/Station	Station or Dock/Dock	Station/Siding	Siding/Dock	Siding/Siding	Total
− 1,400 (53)	− 9,600 (33)	−11,600 (60)	−29,800 (69)	−26,400 (81)	−90,900 (69)
− 2,200 (59)	− 1,300 (71)	− 4,500 (88)	1,900 (106)	40,500 (139)	12,200 (105)
− 1,900 (67)	− 1,400 (90)	− 3,000 (93)	500 (104)	27,600 (134)	− 3,400 (98)
− 3,800 (63)	− 4,600 (69)	200 (100)	4,400 (126)	43,300 (162)	14,800 (106)
− 4,500 (67)	− 1,100 (90)	− 2,500 (97)	4,800 (125)	62,400 (154)	19,600 (105)
− 4,200 (71)	1,800 (121)	2,600 (104)	2,700 (124)	43,600 (139)	10,600 (103)
− 3,500 (78)	1,800 (115)	5,400 (110)	4,100 (143)	36,100 (138)	14,100 (104)
− 4,000 (83)	1,400 (150)	3,300 (112)	1,100 (129)	13,400 (140)	1,900 (101)
−25,500 (72)	−13,100 (84)	−10,100 (97)	−10,400 (95)	240,300 (132)	−21,200 (99)

LOAD—TONS

Station/Station	Station or Dock/Dock	Station/Siding	Siding/Dock	Siding/Siding	Total
7·1	4·7	8·6	13·5	12·8	12·0
5·7	6·2	9·8	10·5	14·6	11·4
6·4	5·8	9·5	6·7	13·3	9·4
8·8	5·3	9·8	9·1	13·2	9·4
4·9	5·0	9·1	7·2	12·2	8·1
3·9	4·5	7·2	6·5	10·9	6·8
4·4	4·5	7·2	5·9	9·4	6·1
4·6	4·2	8·0	5·6	7·9	5·1
5·5	5·1	8·8	11·4	12·7	9·3

apparent discrepancies in totals and margins are due to this.

TABLE V—ANALYSIS BY WAGON LOADING

Combination of terminal conditions (irrespective of the order in which they occur)	Up to 2 tons	Over 2 tons and up to 4 tons	Over 4 tons and up to 6 tons	Over 6 tons and up to 8 tons
				TO
Road–Road　.. 　.. 　..	7,500	9,000	5,000	2,500
Road–Station　.. 　.. 　..	2,900	4,400	2,800	1,900
Road–Dock　.. 　.. 　..	1,700	4,700	4,300	5,500
Road–Siding　.. 　.. 　..	6,600	12,400	14,100	11,600
Station–Station .. 　.. 　..	1,400	2,900	4,500	4,600
Station or Dock–Dock .. 　..	1,100	8,700	5,500	5,300
Station–Siding　.. 　..	3,200	9,800	16,200	14,700
Siding–Dock　.. 　.. 　..	2,200	8,300	13,400	12,200
Siding–Siding　.. 　.. 　..	3,300	12,500	24,200	32,500
TOTAL　.. 　..	29,900	72,800	90,000	91,000
TOTAL WAGONS AND/OR CONTAINERS　.. 　.. 　..	25,400	25,300	18,900	13,800
				MARGIN
Road–Road　.. 　.. 　..	− 42,900 (60)	−14,900　(76)	− 5,100　(79)	− 3,800　(65)
Road–Station　.. 　.. 　..	− 15,400 (57)	− 5,200　(79)	− 2,400　(78)	− 1,400　(79)
Road–Dock　.. 　.. 　..	− 8,300 (53)	− 6,400　(73)	− 5,900　(63)	− 4,500　(68)
Road–Siding　.. 　.. 　..	− 31,600 (60)	−16,000　(76)	−10,800　(80)	− 2,500　(92)
Station–Station .. 　..	− 7,000 (63)	− 2,500　(81)	− 5,600　(65)	− 3,800　(73)
Station or Dock–Dock ..	− 4,200 (54)	− 6,000　(78)	− 1,600　(88)	− 1,100　(91)
Station–Siding　.. 　..	− 13,000 (63)	− 8,800　(78)	− 7,500　(82)	− 200　(99)
Siding–Dock　.. 　..	− 2,700 (72)	− 3,300　(84)	− 4,700　(81)	− 1,200　(92)
Siding–Siding　.. 　..	− 13,300 (60)	− 6,700　(84)	− 4,900　(91)	5,400 (111)
TOTAL　.. 　..	−138,500 (60)	−69,800　(78)	−48,500　(81)	−13,000　(93)
				MARGIN
Road–Road　.. 　..	−5·8	−1·7	−1·0	−1·5
Road–Station　.. 　.. 　..	−5·3	−1·2	−0·9	−0·7
Road–Dock　.. 　.. 　..	−4·9	−1·3	−1·4	−0·8
Road–Siding　.. 　.. 　..	−4·8	−1·3	−0·8	−0·2
Station–Station .. 　.. 　..	−5·0	−0·9	−1·3	−0·8
Station or Dock–Dock .. 　..	−3·9	−0·7	−0·3	−0·2
Station–Siding　.. 　.. 　..	−4·1	−0·9	−0·5	..
Siding–Dock　.. 　.. 　..	−1·2	−0·4	−0·3	−0·1
Siding–Siding　.. 　.. 　..	−4·0	−0·5	−0·2	0·2
	−4·6	−1·0	−0·5	−0·1
MARGIN PER WAGON FORWARDED	−5·4	−2·8	−2·6	−0·9

* The figures in parenthesis show the receipts expressed as a

Note.—All figures have been rounded to the nearest hundred;

Over 8 tons and up to 12 tons	Over 12 tons and up to 16 tons	Over 16 tons and up to 25 tons	Over 25 tons	Total	Total wagons and/or containers forwarded
NS					
2,400	300	100	..	26,800	12,100
4,500	1,000	..	..	17,600	5,700
7,900	1,100	100	100	25,400	5,600
42,600	15,200	7,300	1,700	111,500	21,100
11,100	1,900	3,700	100	30,200	5,500
8,100	3,900	2,300	100	35,000	6,900
82,800	65,600	50,400	3,900	246,600	28,100
54,500	65,000	62,800	37,800	256,300	22,500
196,300	246,400	347,600	83,300	946,000	74,800
410,200	400,500	474,200	126,900	1,695,400	182,400
41,900	29,900	23,500	3,700	182,400	

—£*

Over 8 tons and up to 12 tons	Over 12 tons and up to 16 tons	Over 16 tons and up to 25 tons	Over 25 tons	Total
− 1,600 (81)	− 300 (66)	− 100 (56)	.. (..)	−68,800 (68)
− 2,600 (78)	− 500 (77)	.. (..)	.. (..)	−27,300 (70)
− 5,500 (70)	300 (118)	100 (168)	.. (..)	−30,300 (67)
−15,300 (84)	− 3,300 (90)	2,300 (117)	1,000 (136)	−76,100 (80)
− 6,300 (75)	300 (113)	− 500 (80)	.. (..)	−25,500 (72)
− 1,400 (90)	900 (122)	300 (112)	.. (..)	−13,100 (84)
1,700 (101)	10,000 (115)	4,900 (111)	2,700 (192)	−10,100 (97)
− 7,000 (87)	− 300 (99)	3,600 (112)	5,300 (162)	−10,400 (95)
42,300 (122)	70,600 (140)	114,200 (168)	32,800 (215)	240,300 (132)
4,300 (101)	77,700 (124)	124,800 (148)	41,800 (197)	−21,200 (99)

—£'s PER TON

Over 8 tons and up to 12 tons	Over 12 tons and up to 16 tons	Over 16 tons and up to 25 tons	Over 25 tons	Total	Margin per wagon forwarded
−0·7	−1·0	−1·3	..	−2·6	−5·7
−0·6	−0·4	..	..	−1·6	−4·8
−0·7	0·3	1·1	..	−1·2	−5·4
−0·4	−0·2	0·3	0·6	−0·7	−3·6
−0·6	0·1	−0·1	..	−0·8	−4·6
−0·2	0·2	0·1	..	−0·4	−1·9
..	0·2	0·1	0·7	..	−0·4
−0·1	..	0·1	0·1	..	−0·5
0·2	0·3	0·3	0·4	0·3	3·2
..	0·2	0·3	0·3	..	−0·1
0·1	2·6	5·3	11·3	−0·1	

percentage of direct costs.

apparent discrepancies in totals and margins are due to this.

87

TABLE VI—ANALYSIS BY TRANSIT

	1–25 miles	26–50 miles	51–75 miles	76–100 miles
Wagon-Load Group				WAGONS AND/
Up to 2 tons	1,400	2,200	2,800	2,500
Over 2 and up to 4 tons	3,800	2,900	2,700	2,500
Over 4 and up to 6 tons	3,800	2,400	2,000	2,200
Over 6 and up to 8 tons	3,100	2,000	1,100	1,300
Over 8 and up to 12 tons	12,300	6,300	4,300	4,000
Over 12 and up to 16 tons	9,400	5,100	3,800	3,900
Over 16 and up to 25 tons	7,400	4,700	3,100	2,700
Over 25 tons	1,800	1,100	100	100
TOTAL	43,000	26,600	19,800	19,200
TOTAL TONS	514,300	301,900	186,300	180,600
				MARGIN
Up to 2 tons	− 6,600 (40)	−10,700 (47)	−14,000 (51)	−11,500 (59)
Over 2 and up to 4 tons	−17,300 (35)	−10,500 (59)	− 8,400 (70)	− 5,000 (81)
Over 4 and up to 6 tons	−15,700 (43)	− 7,700 (66)	− 6,000 (75)	− 3,900 (86)
Over 6 and up to 8 tons	− 9,700 (54)	− 4,600 (76)	− 1,900 (85)	− 1,400 (92)
Over 8 and up to 12 tons	−34,000 (61)	− 2,100 (96)	− 1,100 (98)	− 3,600 (94)
Over 12 and up to 16 tons	−16,300 (76)	13,100 (133)	11,300 (130)	18,900 (144)
Over 16 and up to 25 tons	1,500 (103)	21,500 (153)	15,500 (146)	19,200 (158)
Over 25 tons	7,100 (157)	13,000 (239)	1,300 (168)	2,000 (178)
TOTAL	−90,900 (70)	12,200 (105)	− 3,400 (98)	14,800 (106)

* The figures in parenthesis show the receipts

Note.—All figures have been rounded to the nearest hundred;

101–150 miles	151–200 miles	201–300 miles	Over 300 miles	Total	Total Tonnage

OR CONTAINERS

101–150 miles	151–200 miles	201–300 miles	Over 300 miles	Total	Total Tonnage
5,000	5,000	4,400	2,200	25,400	29,900
4,200	4,300	3,300	1,600	25,300	72,800
3,000	2,600	2,000	900	18,900	90,000
2,200	1,600	1,800	700	13,800	91,000
5,600	4,500	3,600	1,500	41,900	410,200
3,800	2,100	1,400	300	29,900	400,500
3,000	1,700	800	200	23,500	474,200
300	100	100	..	3,700	126,900
27,100	21,900	17,300	7,400	182,400	1,695,400
220,600	148,900	105,300	37,500	1,695,400	

—£ *

101–150 miles	151–200 miles	201–300 miles	Over 300 miles	Total	Total Tonnage
−25,800 (59)	−29,500 (60)	−25,800 (65)	−14,600 (70)	−138,500 (60)	
− 9,900 (82)	− 9,600 (85)	− 8,000 (87)	− 1,100 (97)	− 69,800 (78)	
− 6,800 (84)	− 3,600 (92)	− 4,600 (89)	− 200 (99)	− 48,500 (81)	
− 1,100 (97)	1,900 (107)	1,700 (105)	2,100 (111)	− 13,000 (93)	
7,800 (109)	11,600 (115)	17,600 (123)	8,200 (120)	4,300 (101)	
18,200 (132)	13,500 (135)	14,800 (149)	4,100 (137)	77,700 (124)	
29,600 (162)	21,700 (170)	14,100 (170)	1,700 (122)	124,800 (148)	
7,600 (197)	4,700 (221)	4,300 (212)	1,800 (259)	41,800 (197)	
19,600 (105)	10,600 (103)	14,100 (104)	1,900 (101)	− 21,200 (99)	

expressed as a percentage of direct costs.

apparent discrepancies in totals and margins are due to this.

TRAFFIC NOT CARRIED BY RAIL

Minerals and Merchandise

To establish the volume, distance, terminal requirements, and other information relating to traffic not passing by rail, information was collected in all Railway Commercial Districts from all major traders, whether railway customers or not, about regular wagon-load traffic conveyed by any form of transport during 1960.

Where the information was not obtainable from available records, the co-operation of traders estimated to have an annual transport bill of more than £10,000, whether on account of rail, road, water or own 'C' licensed fleet, was sought and found to be readily forthcoming. Other sources of information— British Road Services, British Transport Waterways, British Transport Docks— contributed their quota.

The study covered mineral and general merchandise as one group, and coal and coke as another.

The volume of mineral and merchandise traffic covered by the study was 305 m. tons. Of this, 82 m. tons, or 27 per cent. passed by rail. Within the remaining 223 m. tons there were 93 m. tons of various types of traffic which, by reason of loadability, regularity, distance and terminal requirements, were judged to be potentially favourable to rail.

The distribution of the 93 m. tons of traffic between the methods of transport used was:—

	Million Tons
Conveyed by Road	
Private haulier	37·0
British Road Services ..	7·4
'C' licence or contract 'A'	37·5
Other than by Road	
Sea	7·5
Inland waterways	2·9
Other methods	0·8

Map No. 5 shows the pattern of weekly road distribution of the tonnage considered to be potentially suitable for rail transport. There is a striking similarity between this pattern and that shown by the density map of freight already on rail routes.

The heaviest movement of freight traffic by both road and rail is between the main centres of population, industry, and raw material production, and to and from the major ports. In consequence, the bulk of the movement by road takes place over those parts of the system which are parallel to the more heavily loaded portions of the rail network, and the pattern is one of side-by-side development of the two major forms of transport.

Table No. 23, Section 1, shows how the 223 m. tons not on rail were distributed over different distances. It will be seen that one-half of the total traffic passed over distances of less than 50 miles. Most of this portion, by reason of distance and character, has no rail potential unless the most favourable conditions of terminal and consignment size apply.

ANALYSIS OF NON-RAILBORNE WAGON-LOAD MINERAL AND MERCHANDISE TRAFFIC

Distance gradations (miles)	0–25	26–50	51–100	101–150	151–200	201–300	Over 300	Total
				(million tons)				
SECTION 1								
TONNAGE NOT ON RAIL	62·2	53·6	51·0	29·2	13·1	9·4	4·4	222·9
SECTION 2								
TONNAGE INITIALLY JUDGED FAVOURABLE TO RAIL	6·5	19·7	26·5	18·4	11·6	6·7	3·7	93·1

ANALYSIS BY CONSIGNMENT SIZE AND TERMINAL CONDITIONS
(million tons)

	0–25	26–50	51–100	101–150	151–200	201–300	Over 300	Total
Potential Full Train Loads								
Siding/Siding	0·2	0·7	1·9	3·2	0·7	1·1	0·5	8·3
Siding at one end	0·1	0·6	1·0	0·7	0·7	0·6	0·2	3·9
Siding at neither end	..	0·1	0·1	..	..	..	..	0·2
TOTAL	0·3	1·4	3·0	3·9	1·4	1·7	0·7	12·4
Potential Blocks of Wagons								
Siding/Siding	0·7	0·8	1·5	0·9	0·6	0·5	0·1	5·1
Siding at one end	0·7	2·0	7·4	3·3	1·4	0·6	0·5	15·9
Siding at neither end	..	0·5	1·7	1·7	1·3	0·4	0·2	5·8
TOTAL	1·4	3·3	10·6	5·9	3·3	1·5	0·8	26·8
Wagon Loads								
Siding/Siding	0·4	0·9	1·0	0·5	0·3	0·3	0·2	3·6
Siding at one end	2·5	10·8	8·4	3·7	2·9	1·4	1·1	30·8
Siding at neither end	1·9	3·3	3·5	4·4	3·7	1·8	0·9	19·5
TOTAL	4·8	15·0	12·9	8·6	6·9	3·5	2·2	53·9

		Miles	70–100	101–150	151–200	201–300	Over 300	Total
SECTION 3								
TRAFFIC SUITABLE FOR LINER TRAINS	..	..	2·8	5·6	3·7	2·6	1·0	15·7

91

After the data had been assembled it was sifted and refined to assess what proportions could, in the broad sense, be regarded as having a good rail potential. Bulky and awkward traffic, traffics needing wide dispersal by road, irregular streams—all these and others were deemed to be unsuitable.

In deciding what traffics should be regarded as favourable, loadability, regularity of flow, distance and terminal requirements were all taken into account. The outcome of this first analysis was the 93 m. tons already referred to and its composition by distance is shown in the second line of Table No. 23.

Then, as far as practicable, the consignment sizes and the terminal conditions, which could apply if the traffic passed by rail, were determined. It was particularly desired to establish the volume which could comprise full, or part, train loads and pass under the most favourable terminal conditions. The results are shown in Section 2 of Table No. 23.

It will be seen that the potential volume of traffic in the larger consignment sizes passing under the most favourable rail conditions, i.e., siding/siding, amounts to 13·4 m. tons. There is also 3·9 m. tons of potential full train-load traffic, with siding conditions at one end only, and blocks of traffic, amounting to 15·9 m. tons, with similar conditions. Distance grading may well be the final determining factor as to the rail value of these latter groups as it is only in the higher ranges, 150 miles and above, that a margin over direct costs can be expected.

All traffic embraced in the 93 m. tons, and moving more than 70 miles, was assessed as to its suitability for Liner Train conveyance. Estimates of the potential tonnage, in distance ranges, are shown in Section 3 of the table. Out of the 15·7 m. tons, two-thirds would be drawn from wagon-load traffic where there would not be a siding at either end. The balance is drawn from traffic which could have terminal conditions involving a siding.

Further studies of the potential will be made to determine whether there remains, within the 130 m. tons discarded originally, any more traffic of Liner Train potential. Some traffics, by reason of fragility or other characteristics, might have been judged unsuitable in the earlier stages.

Coal, Coke and Patent Fuels

A similar study carried out with the full co-operation of the National Coal Board, merchants, and traders, covered 209 m. tons of fuel of which 150 m. tons passed by rail. The balance—59 m. tons—was carried by private lines, sea, waterways, and road, or by a combination of some of these means.

Map No. 6 shows the volume and geographical distribution of fuel conveyed by road, canal and coastwise. A substantial proportion of the traffic passing coastwise is carried to the ports by rail, a combination of function which is probably the most suitable and economic.

A distance analysis of the coal conveyed by road, showing the proportion regarded as favourable to rail, is shown in the following table. It will be seen that by far the greater volume on road, some 20 m. tons, or 64 per cent. of the total, passes over distances less than 25 miles.

Table No. 24

COAL PASSING BY ROAD, ANALYSED BY DISTANCE GRADATION

Distance Gradations (miles)

	0–25	26–50	50-100	101–150	151–200	Total
			(million tons)			
(A) Total traffic	19·6	6·3	3·7	0·7	0·3	30·6
(B) Favourable to rail traffic	8·1	4·7	3·4	0·7	0·3	17·1

Apparent discrepancies in totals are due to rounding.

The volume of coal on road and suitable for rail conveyance is such that a high proportion, 69 per cent. would comprise through train-loads, or part loads, for one destination if assembled at the marshalling yards immediately serving the originating collieries. The balance, 31 per cent., would require to pass through more than one yard. Table No. 25 shows the division of the 17 m. tons.

The setting up of coal concentration points, and any reduction in the number of collieries serving both them and larger individual receivers, could lead to a substantial increase in direct working from colliery to destination.

Table No. 25

FAVOURABLE TO RAIL COAL TRAFFIC PASSING BY ROAD, ANALYSED BY BROAD CONSIGNMENT SIZE AND TERMINAL CONDITIONS

Terminal conditions	Through train-loads	Block Wagon-loads	Wagon-loads	Total
		(million tons)		
Siding/Siding	3·9	4·7	1·7	10·2
Siding at forwarding end ..	—	3·2	3·7	7·0
Other	—	—	—	—
TOTAL	3·9	7·9	5·4	17·1

Apparent discrepancies in totals are due to rounding.

FREIGHT SUNDRIES TRAFFIC

To determine the volume, distribution and composition of sundries traffic throughout the country, a test was made of all traffic passing on one day.

For the purpose of costing traffic, terminal and other operations were studied, recorded, and costed over one week.

Arising out of this investigation the annual volume and certain characteristics of sundries traffic were assessed under:—

		millions
Tons		3·4
Consignments		43
Packages		177
Loaded wagons forwarded		3·7

93

Average weights and number of packages in each consignment on the test day were recorded as being:—

Consignment weight	178 lb.
Package weight	43 lb.
Packages per consignment	4·1
Originating weight per loaded wagon forwarded ..	0·92 tons

An analysis of consignments by weight is given in the following table:—

Table No. 26

Weight group	Percentage of total	Average number of packages per consignment
	(Figures in brackets are cumulative)	
Under 1 qr.	13	1·2
1 and under 2 qrs.	27 (40)	1·4
2 and under 3 qrs.	14 (54)	2·0
3 and under 1 cwt.	8 (62)	2·8
1 and under 2 cwt.	17 (79)	3·8
2 and under 3 cwt.	7 (86)	5·9
3 and under 5 cwt.	6 (92)	8·8
5 and under 10 cwt. ..	5 (97)	14·6
10 and over	3 (100)	20·1
	100	

Based on the study and detailed costing, the annual receipts were estimated to be £36 m. and the direct costs £47 m., a loss of £11 m., taking no account of indirect expenses or interest charges.

There are 550 rail stations operating as railheads for sundries traffic now. Collection and delivery services are based on them. Four hundred other stations, mostly small ones in sparsely populated country, handle small amounts.

Distribution of traffic over the 950 stations is set out in the following table:—

Table No. 27

Tonnage handled daily	Stations		Volume	
	Number	Percentage of total	Tons	Percentage of total
	(Figures in brackets are cumulative)			
1–25	698	73	4,581	17
26–50	121	13 (86)	4,232	16 (33)
51–100	66	7 (93)	4,540	17 (50)
101–200	39	4 (97)	5,236	20 (70)
201–300	16	2 (99)	4,143	15 (85)
301 and above	10	1 (100)	4,090	15 (100)
TOTAL	950	100	26,822	100

Over a period of seven years the tonnage of sundries traffic has declined as shown:—

Year			Tons
1954	..	..	5·5 m.
1960	..	..	3·6 m.
1961–2	..	..	3·4 m.

Consequently, the opportunity to make direct loads diminishes. This leads to increase in transhipment, which increases costs and extends transit times. It is estimated that on average the total volume of sundries—3·4 m. tons—is loaded into and unloaded from rail wagons at least twice.

Hitherto the pattern of sundries working throughout the country has been by hand-stowing in, and unloading from, 12-ton covered vans, with increasing frequency and radius of road collection and delivery as towns expanded. There has also been a willingness to serve almost every hamlet and no effective restriction, through charging or other means, on the nature of consignments carried, however awkward they might be.

The pattern of movement of railborne sundries traffic is shown in Map No. 7. As might be expected, it follows closely that of full load traffic and the movement of traffic by road.

If the Railway is to remain in the business of carrying freight sundries then it must be made to pay, and the study has shown that this objective may be achieved by a combination of cost reduction and charges revision. Reductions in cost should be attainable by:—

(1) Reduction in the number of places at which the traffic is handled.

(2) Reduction in the volume transhipped.

(3) Development and extended use of mechanical appliances.

(4) Overhaul of cartage operations.

(5) Greater use of containers and pallets.

(6) Planned freight services following the Liner Train principle.

(7) Simplified documentation.

From this study there has already emerged the outline of a National Plan which can be adopted, once it has been established, through the investigations now in progress, that the business can be made viable.

The problems of transhipment are being studied. Investigations into the possibility of extending mechanical handling are proceeding. The need for so much documentation is being examined.

Subject to further study, and decision on the extent to which it is worth-while staying in some parts of the business, it is envisaged that the number of main depots will ultimately be in the region of 100. As would be expected, they should be located on, or near to, the more densely occupied routes, and the anticipated locations are shown on Map. No. 8.

The capital expenditure envisaged might be of the order of £11 m. Possible reduction in working costs has been assessed at £20 m. Use of containers and the movement of sundries by Liner Trains could further improve the position and attract new traffic.

An Officer has been assigned full-time to development of all aspects of the plan on a national scale.

PASSENGER SERVICE, LINE AND STATION CLOSURES

Section 1—Passenger Services to be Withdrawn.

Section 2—Passenger Services to be Modified.

Section 3—Passenger Stations and Halts to be Closed—England.

Section 4—Passenger Stations and Halts to be Closed—Scotland.

Section 5—Passenger Stations and Halts to be Closed—Wales.

Section 6—Passenger Services already under Consideration for Withdrawal before the Formulation of the Report.

Section 7—Passenger Stations and Halts already under Consideration for Closure before the Formulation of the Report—England.

Section 8—Passenger Stations and Halts already under Consideration for Closure before the Formulation of the Report—Scotland.

Section 9—Passenger Stations and Halts already under Consideration for Closure before the Formulation of the Report—Wales.

PASSENGER SERVICE, LINE AND STATION CLOSURES

As soon as the required procedure permits, it is desired to withdraw those passenger train services which are clearly uneconomic. The procedure to be followed is laid down in Section 56 of the Transport Act, 1962. Schedules of the services to be withdrawn or modified, including those which were under consideration in August 1962 and have since been withdrawn in part, are given in Sections 1, 2 and 6 of this Appendix. Other Sections give lists, in alphabetical order, of the stations and halts which, as a consequence, will be closed to passengers.

In most cases there will eventually be no passenger service of any description over the lines affected. In others, fast and semi-fast services using the same routes will continue to run. In still other cases it is intended to modify the pattern of services, both stopping and fast, in ways which will reduce the train mileage and cut out the more uneconomic portions of services and under-utilised stations.

The number of stations and halts which will be closed is 2,363, including 435 under consideration before the Report appeared. Of these, 235 have already been closed. Services will be completely withdrawn from about 5,000 route miles. The extent of the complete withdrawals is shown on Map No. 9. When services are to be modified, these are shown on Map No. 10. Changes proposed in the London area are shown on Map No. 9A.

Comparisons with passenger density Map No. 1, and with Map No. 3 giving density by station receipts, show the extent to which the proposed withdrawals and modifications are related to the least used lines and stations.

These proposals do not include all the stopping passenger services now running. Reshaping and streamlining the pattern of these services must be a continuing process. As this proceeds other services and stations will be added to the withdrawal and modification lists until a point is reached when what remains can be said to be viable.

Examples of the assessments made of the annual revenue and expenses, associated with a variety of passenger services, are given in Table No. 1, and in the following paragraphs particular services, and their contribution, have been described in some detail.

Gleneagles–Crieff–Comrie

This is a rural service of ten trains a day in each direction. There is an element of summer holiday traffic. The service is operated by diesel rail bus on weekdays only over a distance of 15 miles. Connections are made at Gleneagles with main line trains to and from Glasgow and Edinburgh. The stations served are:—

Gleneagles	Highlandman
Tullibardine	Pittenzie Halt
Muthill	Crieff
Strageath Halt	Comrie

All stations except Gleneagles would be closed to passengers.

Some 340,000 passenger miles accrue to this service which accounts for 65,000 train miles a year. On average, there are 5 passengers on a train at any one time. Earnings are £1,900 and these represent little more than a quarter of the train movement expenses of £7,500. Station terminal expenses bring the total of direct expenses to nearly £11,000, less than a fifth of which is covered by the earnings of the service. When track and signalling expenses are added—£8,200—the total expenses are ten times as great as the earnings of the service.

Passengers using this service in combination with other services contribute more than £12,000 to the earnings of other rail services, and it is estimated that withdrawal of the service would result in the loss of £9,000 of this contributory revenue. Because there would be no alternative rail service on this line after withdrawal, none of the earnings on the service would be retained.

Despite the estimate of contributory loss, which is probably high, bearing in mind that holidaymakers may travel elsewhere, the overall net financial improvement expected from withdrawal is nearly £8,400, or more than two-fifths of the present level of total direct expenses attributable to the service.

Thetford–Swaffham

This is a rural branch service covering 23 route miles and connecting at Thetford with main line services from Liverpool Street. The stations served are:—

Thetford	Wretham and Hockham
Stow Bedon	Holme Hale
Watton	Swaffham

Thetford and Swaffham would remain open after withdrawal of the service. On weekdays, five trains a day in each direction are worked by diesel multiple units over the whole route, and one a day between Thetford and Watton.

The train miles are 86,000 and, on average, there are 9 passengers on a train. The earnings are £3,700, the movement expenses amount to £13,200, and the terminal expenses to a further £3,900.

The shortfall of earnings on the movement and terminal expenses is £13,400, equivalent to more than three-quarters of these expenses. In addition, the track and signalling expenses which could be saved by the withdrawal of the service amount to £17,200, increasing the shortfall to £30,600. Put another way, the earnings on the service cover roughly one-tenth of the total direct expenses.

The gross revenue accruing to other services, contributed by passengers using the Thetford–Swaffham service on part of their rail journey, amounts to some £16,000. Allowance must be made for the loss of £1,700 of this contributory revenue and, taking this into account, it is estimated that the loss in gross revenue will be £5,400.

The estimated net financial improvement in revenue which would result from the withdrawal of the service amounts to about £29,000, equivalent to over four-fifths of the total direct expenses.

Hull–York via Beverley

This is a stopping service over a distance of 42 miles, serving a rural area between the cities of Hull and York, and with an element of commuter traffic at each end. The stations served are:—

Hull	Londesborough
Cottingham	Pocklington
Beverley	Stamford Bridge
Kipling Cotes	Earswick
Market Weighton	York

All intermediate stations except Cottingham and Beverley would be closed.

Nine trains run in each direction on weekdays and most of them are composed of diesel multiple units.

In a year the service involves 260,000 train miles. On average, there are 57 passengers on a train. The earnings of the service are £90,400, and cover the movement expenses of £84,400. Terminal expenses bring the total of movement and terminal expenses to £107,500, so that earnings show a shortfall of £17,100. It is estimated that withdrawal of the service would reduce track and signalling expenses by £43,300. Thus, on total direct expenses of £150,800, earnings show a shortfall of £60,400, equivalent to two-fifths of total direct expenses.

Because alternative services would be available after withdrawal of the service, £25,600 of the present earnings would be retained. It is estimated that passengers using the service as part of their rail journey contribute £37,700 to the revenue of other services. Because of the existence of services between Hull and York via other routes, only £4,900 of this amount is expected to be lost.

The total loss in gross revenue resulting from withdrawal of the service is estimated at £69,700, but the overall net financial improvement is expected to be £81,000, equivalent to over half of the total direct expenses.

(87549)

G*2

Region	Service	Traction	Type of service	Route miles	Train miles	Earnings £	
					'000	Total	Expected to be lost
North-Eastern	Hull–York (via Beverley) ..	Diesel/ DMU	Rural/ commuter	42	259·7	90,400	64,790
Scottish	Banff–Tillynaught	Steam	Rural	6	37·4	800	800
North-Eastern	Bradford and Leeds to Skipton (via Ilkley)	DMU	Commuter/ rural/ holiday	26 and 28	404·2	59,700	59,000
Eastern	Thetford–Swaffham	DMU	Rural	23	86·1	3,700	3,700
Western	Chippenham–Calne	DMU	Rural	5	48·6	4,700	4,700
Western	Yatton–Clevedon	DMU	Commuter	4	46·6	6,100	6,100
Scottish	Elgin–Lossiemouth	Diesel	Rural	6	11·2	625	625
North-Eastern	Sunderland–West Hartlepool ..	DMU	Inter-urban	18	38·4	8,500	5,300
Scottish	Aberdeen–Ballater	Battery car/ DMU	Rural/ commuter/ holiday	43	161·0	14,370	14,370
Scottish	Gleneagles–Crieff–Comrie ..	Diesel rail bus	Holiday/ rural	15	65·1	1,900	1,900

The heavy vertical lines indicate the stage in the relationship between revenue and expenses
The direct track and signalling expenses shown above are the additional expenses

EFFECT OF WITHDRAWING TYPICAL PASSENGER SERVICES

Contributory gross revenue £		Expected loss in total gross revenue £	Movement expenses			Net financial effect based on movement expenses £	Terminal expenses £	Total movement and terminal expenses £	Net financial effect based on total movement and terminal expenses £	Direct track and signalling expenses £	Net financial effect based on total direct expenses £
Total	Expected to be lost		Total £	Per train mile s. d.							
37,680	4,900	69,690	84,400	6 6		+14,710	23,100	107,500	+37,810	43,300	+81,110
6,130	4,000	4,800	14,150	7 7		+ 9,350	950	15,100	+10,300	600	+10,900
24,370	5,930	64,930	73,900	3 8		+ 8,970	31,600	105,500	+40,570	48,400	+88,970
16,000	1,700	5,400	13,200	3 1		+ 7,800	3,900	17,100	+11,700	17,200	+28,900
56,900	5,700	10,400	15,500	6 5		+ 5,100	8,900	24,400	+14,000	10,000	+24,000
22,200	1,100	7,200	11,500	4 11		+ 4,300	5,600	17,100	+ 9,900	8,000	+17,900
18,330	370	1,000	3,150	5 7		+ 2,150	1,500	4,650	+ 3,650	1,800	+ 5,450
3,370	170	5,470	7,400	3 10		+ 1,930	3,300	10,700	+ 5,230	..	+ 5,230
21,980	7,000	21,370	19,850	2 6		− 1,520	9,250	29,100	+ 7,730	20,980	+28,710
12,280	9,000	10,900	7,500	2 4		− 3,400	3,480	10,980	+ 80	8,280	+ 8,360

at which withdrawal of the service becomes financially justified.
incurred in providing track and signalling to passenger train standards for the services concerned.

PASSENGER SERVICE, LINE AND STATION CLOSURES
Passenger Services to be Withdrawn

Glasgow Central–Carlisle (Local)
Edinburgh Princes Street–Carstairs–Lanark
Glasgow St. Enoch–Dumfries–Carlisle (Local)
Glasgow St. Enoch–Lugton–Kilmarnock (Local)
Darvel–Kilmarnock
Stranraer–Dumfries
Dumfries–Castle Douglas–Kirkcudbright
Glasgow St. Enoch–Dalry–Kilmarnock
Ayr–Dalmellington
Kilmarnock–Ayr
Kilmarnock–Ardrossan
Lanark–Muirkirk
Glasgow Central–Edinburgh Princes Street
Hamilton–Strathaven/Coalburn
Edinburgh Waverley–Berwick-upon-Tweed (Local)
Edinburgh Waverley–Dunbar
Edinburgh Waverley–Hawick–Carlisle
Langholm–Riddings Junction–Carlisle
Thornton–Crail–Dundee
Stirling–Alloa–Kinross
Glasgow Buchanan Street–Stirling–Perth (Local)
Gleneagles–Crieff–Comrie
Glasgow Buchanan Street–Stirling–Oban
Killin Junction–Killin
Oban–Connel Ferry–Ballachulish
Craigendoran–Arrochar
Fort William–Mallaig (Local)
Ballinluig–Aberfeldy
Perth–Blair Atholl–Struan
Lossiemouth–Elgin
Aberdeen–Inverurie
Aberdeen–Keith–Elgin (Local)
Aberdeen–Fraserburgh
Maud–Peterhead
Fraserburgh–St. Combs
Tillynaught–Banff
Aberdeen–Ballater
Aviemore–Craigellachie–Elgin

Aviemore–Inverness–Elgin (Local)
Georgemas Junction–Thurso
Glasgow St. Enoch–Barrhead
Glasgow St. Enoch–East Kilbride
Glasgow St. Enoch–Kilmacolm
Glasgow St. Enoch–Paisley West
Coatbridge–Dumbarton
Edinburgh Princes Street–Kingsknowe
Glasgow Queen Street–Kirkintilloch
Edinburgh Waverley–Musselburgh
Ayr–Stranraer
Inverness–Wick
Inverness–Kyle of Lochalsh
Doncaster–Leeds Central (Local)
Selby–Goole
York–Hull
Hull–Hornsea Town
Hull–Withernsea
Driffield–Selby
Leeds Central–Castleford Central–Pontefract
Leeds City–Knottingley
Wakefield–Goole
Bradford Exchange–Batley–Wakefield
Leeds Central–Pudsey–Bradford Exchange
Bradford Exchange–Mirfield–Huddersfield (Local)
Bradford Exchange–Halifax–Huddersfield (Local)
Huddersfield–Clayton West–Penistone
Leeds City and Bradford Forster Square–Ilkley–Skipton
Leeds City and Bradford Forster Square–Keighley–Skipton (Local)
Leeds City–Shipley–Bradford Forster Square (Local)
Leeds City–Cudworth–Sheffield Midland (Local)
Leeds City–Cross Gates–Micklefield (Local)
Leeds City–Wetherby–Harrogate
Wetherby–Church Fenton
Malton–Whitby
Middlesbrough–Guisborough
Middlesbrough–Whitby–Scarborough
York–Harrogate
Leeds–Harrogate–Northallerton–Darlington
Darlington–Richmond
Darlington–Barnard Castle–Middleton-in-Teesdale
Darlington–Bishop Auckland–Crook
Sunderland–Durham–Bishop Auckland
Sunderland–West Hartlepool (Local)
Newcastle-on-Tyne–Washington
Sunderland–South Shields
Newcastle-on-Tyne–Hexham (Local)
Newcastle-on-Tyne–Haltwhistle (Local)
Newcastle-on-Tyne–Newbiggin
Newsham–Blyth

Monkseaton–Blyth–Newbiggin
Newcastle-on-Tyne–Riverside–Tynemouth (Local)
York–Sheffield Victoria–Nottingham Victoria–Leicester Central–Banbury
Crewe–Warrington–Preston–Carlisle (Local)
Dunstable North–Hatfield
Wolverton–Newport Pagnell
Buckingham–Bletchley
Northampton Castle–Peterborough East
Wellingborough Midland Road–Northampton Castle
Seaton–Stamford
Rugby Midland–Peterborough East
Leamington Spa Avenue–Coventry–Nuneaton Trent Valley
Derby Midland–Tamworth–Birmingham New Street (Local)
Wolverhampton High Level–Burton-on-Trent
Wellington–Shrewsbury (Local)
Stafford–Wellington
Crewe–Shrewsbury (Local)
Crewe–Chester General (Local)
Bangor–Afon Wen
Chester General–Holyhead/Caernarvon (Local)
Manchester Exchange–Warrington Bank Quay–Chester General (Local)
Llandudno–Blaenau Ffestiniog
Bangor–Amlwch
Wrexham Central–Chester Northgate–New Brighton
Liverpool Lime Street–Chester General
Manchester Piccadilly–Buxton
Stoke-on-Trent–Silverdale
Kidsgrove–Etruria (Stoke Loop)
Leek–Uttoxeter
Stockport Edgeley–Stalybridge (Local)
Liverpool Lime Street–Tyldesley–Patricroft–Manchester Exchange (Local)
St. Helens Shaw Street–Earlestown–Warrington Bank Quay
Manchester Exchange–Huddersfield (Local)
Wigan Wallgate–Fazakerley–Liverpool Exchange
Wigan Central–Glazebrook
Glazebrook–Stockport Tiviot Dale
Blackpool North–Fleetwood
Manchester Victoria–Bury–Bacup
Manchester Victoria–Bury–Accrington–Colne
Southport Chapel Street–Preston
Earby–Barnoldswick
Rose Grove–Todmorden
Sellafield–Moor Row
Ulverston–Lake Side (Windermere)
Barrow–Whitehaven
Carlisle–Penrith–Workington
Oxenholme–Windermere (Local)
Carlisle–Silloth
Kettering–Leicester London Road (Local)
Leicester London Road–Nottingham Midland (Local)

Manchester Central–Chinley–Derby Midland (Local)
Buxton–Miller's Dale
Banbury–Woodford Halse
Manchester Central–Chinley–Hope–Sheffield Midland
Kettering–Melton Mowbray–Nottingham Midland
Nottingham Midland–Melton Mowbray
Leicester London Road–Burton-on-Trent
Leicester–Peterborough North
Leicester London Road–Melton Mowbray
Derby Friar Gate–Nottingham Victoria
Derby Midland–Trent–Nottingham Midland (Local)
Nottingham Midland–Worksop
Derby Midland–Sheffield Midland (Local)
Carnforth–Wennington
Carlisle–Skipton
London Broad Street–Richmond
Watford Junction–Croxley Green
Harrow and Wealdstone–Belmont
Watford Junction–St. Albans Abbey
Walsall–Rugeley Trent Valley
Birmingham New Street–Sutton Park–Walsall
Walsall–Dudley
Manchester Exchange–Tyldesley–Wigan North Western (Local)
Manchester Exchange–Stalybridge–Greenfield
Manchester Victoria–Newton Heath–Middleton
Manchester Victoria–Horwich
Liverpool Lime Street–St. Helens–Wigan North Western
Manchester Victoria–Bury Bolton Street
Royton–Royton Junction
Southport Chapel Street–Crossens
Liverpool Exchange–Southport Chapel Street
Lancaster Castle/Lancaster Green Ayre–Heysham
Manchester Piccadilly–Hadfield/Glossop
Manchester Piccadilly–Romiley–Hayfield/Macclesfield
London St. Pancras–Barking (Local)
London Marylebone–Leicester Central–Nottingham Victoria
Westerfield–Yarmouth South Town
Shelford–Marks Tey
Saxmundham–Aldeburgh
Audley End–Bartlow
Cambridge–St. Ives–March
Swaffham–Thetford
Dereham–Wells-Next-The-Sea
Sheringham–Melton Constable
North Walsham–Mundesley-on-Sea
Lincoln Central–Woodhall Junction–Firsby
Firsby–Skegness
Willoughby–Mablethorpe
Lincoln St. Marks–Nottingham Midland
Barton-on-Humber–New Holland Town

New Holland Pier–Cleethorpes (Local)
Sheffield Midland–Nottingham Midland (Local)
St. Margarets–Buntingford
Romford–Upminster
Witham (Essex)–Maldon East and Heybridge
Witham (Essex)–Braintree and Bocking
Wivenhoe–Brightlingsea
Peterborough North–Spalding–Grimsby Town
Patney and Chirton–Holt Junction
Chippenham–Calne
Bath Green Park–Bournemouth West
Bristol Temple Meads–Bath Green Park
Taunton–Yeovil Pen Mill
Taunton–Minehead
Tiverton Junction–Tiverton
Taunton–Barnstaple Junction
Liskeard–Looe
Lostwithiel–Fowey
St. Erth–St. Ives (Cornwall)
Kemble–Cirencester Town
Kemble–Tetbury
Gloucester Central–Hereford
Porth–Maerdy
Abercynon–Aberdare
Barry–Bridgend
Cardiff–Coryton
Caerphilly–Senghenydd
Bridgend–Treherbert
Carmarthen–Aberystwyth
Berkeley Road–Sharpness
Worcester Shrub Hill–Bromyard
Swan Village–Great Bridge
Old Hill–Dudley
Whitchurch (Salop)–Welshpool
Ruabon–Morfa Mawddach/Barmouth
Bala–Bala Junction
Llanymynech–Llanfyllin
West Drayton and Yiewsley–Staines West
Bristol Temple Meads–Portishead
Bristol Temple Meads–Avonmouth Dock
Yatton–Clevedon
Bristol Temple Meads–Patchway–Pilning
Bristol Temple Meads–Clifton Down–Pilning
Cardiff Clarence Road–Cardiff General
Ashford (Kent)–Hastings
Ashford (Kent)–New Romney
Crowhurst–Bexhill West
Haywards Heath–Seaford (Local)
Three Bridges–Tunbridge Wells West
Tonbridge–Brighton

Tonbridge–Eastbourne
Brighton–Horsham *
Guildford–Horsham
Maiden Newton–Bridport
Brockenhurst–Ringwood–Bournemouth
Salisbury–Fordingbridge–Bournemouth
Okehampton–Plymouth
Barnstaple Junction–Ilfracombe
Okehampton–Padstow
Okehampton–Bude
Barnstaple Junction–Torrington
Yeovil Junction–Yeovil Town
Chard Central–Chard Junction
Axminster–Lyme Regis
Seaton Junction–Seaton (Devon)
Sidmouth Junction–Sidmouth
Tipton St. John's–Exmouth
Exeter Central–Exmouth
Bere Alston–Callington
Halwill–Torrington
Bodmin Road/Bodmin North–Wadebridge–Padstow
Ryde Pier Head–Ventnor/Cowes
Winchester City–Alton
Portsmouth–Botley–Romsey/Andover
Portsmouth–Netley–Southampton-Romsey/Andover (Local)
Romsey–Andover
Reading Southern–Guildford–Redhill–Tonbridge (Local)
Clapham Junction–Kensington Olympia

Section 2

PASSENGER SERVICE, LINE AND STATION CLOSURES
Passenger Services to be Modified

Newcastle-on-Tyne–Berwick-upon-Tweed
Hull–Selby–Leeds City
Hull–Bridlington–Scarborough
Leeds City–Morecambe–Heysham
York–Wakefield Kirkgate–Sowerby Bridge–Manchester Victoria
Newcastle-on-Tyne–Carlisle
Alnmouth–Alnwick
Oxford–Bletchley–Cambridge
Birmingham New Street–Barnt Green
Wrexham General–Chester General–Birkenhead Woodside
Manchester Piccadilly–Macclesfield–Stoke-on-Trent
Crewe–Derby Midland
Manchester Victoria–Rochdale–Todmorden
Bolton Trinity Street–Bury Knowsley Street–Rochdale
Manchester Victoria–Wigan Wallgate–Southport Chapel Street
Liverpool Central–Manchester Central
Liverpool Central–Gateacre–Warrington Central
Blackpool Central–Manchester/East Lancashire
Liverpool Exchange–Ormskirk–Blackpool Central
Carnforth–Barrow

Birmingham New Street–Leicester London Road–Nottingham Midland
Derby Midland–Nottingham Midland
London Euston–Watford Junction
London Broad Street–Watford Junction
Birmingham New Street–Sutton Coldfield–Lichfield City
Birmingham New Street–Redditch
Manchester Oxford Road–Crewe
Manchester Victoria–Rochdale/Oldham
London St. Pancras–Nottingham Midland
Ipswich–Norwich (Local)
Cambridge–Ely–King's Lynn
Bishops Stortford–Cambridge
Ely–Norwich
Cambridge–Ipswich
Ely–Newmarket
Norwich–Dereham–King's Lynn
Norwich–Sheringham
Grantham–Boston
Grantham–Nottingham
Lincoln Central–Market Rasen–Cleethorpes
Didcot–Swindon
Swindon–Bath Spa–Bristol Temple Meads
Bristol Temple Meads–Taunton
Chippenham–Trowbridge–Westbury (Wilts.)
Reading General–Westbury (Wilts.)
Bristol Temple Meads–Bath Spa–Westbury (Wilts.)–Weymouth Town
Taunton–Exeter St. Davids
Exeter St. Davids–Kingswear
Plymouth–Penzance
Par–Newquay (Cornwall)
Cardiff General–Carmarthen
Carmarthen–Neyland/Milford Haven
Carmarthen–Fishguard Harbour
Swindon–Kemble–Gloucester Central
Cheltenham Spa–Cardiff General
Whitland–Pembroke Dock
Didcot–Oxford–Leamington Spa
Oxford–Worcester Shrub Hill
Stratford-on-Avon–Honeybourne
Stourbridge–Worcester–Hereford
Birmingham New Street–Worcester Shrub Hill
Worcester Shrub Hill–Gloucester Eastgate
Gloucester Eastgate–Bristol Temple Meads
Shrewsbury–Welshpool–Aberystwyth
Tunbridge Wells Central–Hastings
Sheerness-on-Sea–Dover Priory (Local)
Brighton–Ore (Local)
Basingstoke–Salisbury
Salisbury–Exeter Central
Exeter Central–Okehampton
Exeter Central–Barnstaple Junction

PASSENGER SERVICE, LINE AND STATION CLOSURES

Passenger Stations and Halts to be Closed

ENGLAND

Abbey Town
Acrow Halt
Acton Central
Addingham
Adlestrop
Ainsdale
Airmyn
Aldeburgh
Aldermaston
Aldridge
Alford Town (Lincs.)
Alfreton and South Normanton
Alresford (Hants.)
Alrewas
Altofts and Whitwood
Alton Towers
Ambergate
Andover Town
Apperley Bridge
Appleby (Westmorland)
Appledore (Kent)
Ardsley
Ardwick
Armathwaite
Armley Canal Road
Armley Moor
Arram
Arthington
Ascott-under-Wychwood
Ashbury
Ashburys for Belle Vue
Ashby-de-la-Zouch
Ashby Magna
Ashcott
Ashdon Halt
Ashey (Isle of Wight)
Ashington
Ashley Heath Halt
Ashley Hill
Ashperton
Ashton Charlestown
Ashton Gate
Ashwater
Ashwell
Askham

Aspley Guise
Athelney
Avoncliff Halt
Avonmouth Dock
Awsworth
Aynho for Deddington

Bacup
Baguley
Bagworth and Ellistown
Bailey Gate
Ballingham
Balshaw Lane and Euxton
Bamford
Bank Hall
Banks
Baptist End Halt
Barcombe Mills
Bardney
Bardon Mill
Bardsey
Barlow
Barnard Castle
Barnoldswick
Barnstaple Town
Barnwell
Barrow Haven
Barrow-on-Soar and Quorn
Bartlow
Barton-on-Humber
Basford North
Bason Bridge
Bassenthwaite Lake
Bath Green Park
Bathampton
Bathford Halt
Battersby
Baynards
Bebside
Beccles
Bedlington
Bedworth
Bedwyn
Beechburn
Beeston Castle and Tarporley

Belmont (Middx.)
Belper
Ben Rhydding
Bentham
Bere Alston
Bere Ferrers
Berkeley
Berkeley Road
Berry Brow
Berwick (Sussex)
Besses-o'-th'-Barn
Betchworth
Bexhill West
Bickershaw and Abram
Bideford
Binegar
Birch Vale
Birkdale
Birkenhead Woodside
Bishop Auckland
Bishop's Lydeard
Bishop's Nympton and Molland
Bishopstone
Bitton
Blaby
Black Dog Halt
Blackdyke Halt
Blackhall Colliery
Black Horse Road
Blackpool North
Blackrod
Blackwell
Blacon
Blaisdon Halt
Blandford Forum
Blaydon
Bleadon and Uphill Halt
Bleasby
Blencow
Bletchington
Blockley
Bloxwich
Blue Anchor
Blundellsands and Crosby
Blyth
Bodmin General
Bodmin North
Bollington
Bolton Abbey
Bolton-le-Sands
Bolton Percy
Bootle (Cumberland)

Bootle Oriel Road
Borrowash
Botanic Gardens
Botley
Boughton Halt
Bow (Devon)
Bow Brickhill
Bowker Vale
Box
Box Mill Lane
Brackley Central
Bradford Peverell and Stratton Halt
Brading (Isle of Wight)
Bradwell (Bucks)
Braintree and Bocking
Braithwaite
Bramber
Bramley and Wonersh
Brampton (Suffolk)
Brancepeth
Brandon Colliery
Bransford Road
Braughing
Braunton
Braystones
Breamore
Bredon
Brent (Devon)
Brent Knoll
Brentor
Bricket Wood
Bridestowe
Bridport
Brigham
Brightlingsea
Brimscombe
Broadbottom
Broad Clyst
Broad Green
Broadstone
Brockholes
Bromfield
Bromham and Rowde Halt
Brompton (Yorks.)
Bromyard
Brondesbury
Brondesbury Park
Brookland Halt
Broomfleet
Broomielaw
Brownhills
Bruton

Bryn
Buckingham
Bude
Budleigh Salterton
Bugle
Bulwell Market
Buntingford
Bures
Burgh-by-Sands
Burgh-le-Marsh
Burlescombe
Burley-in-Wharfedale
Burslem
Burton Agnes
Burton Joyce
Bury Bolton Street
Buxted
Buxton

Cadishead
Callington
Calne
Calstock
Calverley and Rodley
Camelford
Cannock
Carbis Bay
Carcroft and Adwick-le-Street
Carlton and Netherfield
Carnaby
Carville
Castle Ashby and Earls Barton
Castleford Cutsyke
Castlethorpe
Castleton (Yorks.)
Cattal
Catterick Bridge
Cattistock Halt
Causeland Halt
Cavendish
Chacewater
Chalford
Challow
Chandlers Ford
Chapel-en-le-Frith Central
Chapel-en-le Frith South
Chapelton
Chappel and Wake's Colne
Chard Junction
Charfield

Charlbury
Chatteris
Cheadle (Cheshire)
Cheadle Heath
Cheddleton
Cheltenham Spa Malvern Road
Chester-le-Street
Chester Northgate
Chesterton Lane Halt
Chetnole Halt
Chilcompton
Chilsworthy
Chilvers Coton
Chilworth and Albury
Chipping Campden
Chittening Platform
Chorlton-cum-Hardy
Christian Malford Halt
Churchdown
Church's Hill Halt
Churchtown
Churston
Cirencester Town
Clapham (Yorks.)
Clare
Clatford
Clay Cross
Claydon (Bucks.)
Clayton Bridge
Clayton West
Cleckheaton
Clevedon
Clifton Bridge
Clifton Down
Clough Fold
Cloughton
Coaley
Coalville Town
Cobridge
Cockermouth for Buttermere
Codnor Park and Ironville
Cole
Collingham
Collingham Bridge
Colnbrook
Colnbrook Estate Halt
Colyford
Colyton
Combe Halt
Combpyne

Commondale
Coningsby
Cononley
Consall
Cooksbridge
Coombe Junction Halt
Copplestone
Coppull
Corbridge
Corby
Corkickle
Corsham
Corton
Cotherstone
Coundon Road
County School
Cowes (Isle of Wight)
Cox Green
Cranleigh
Creech St. Michael Halt
Creekmoor Halt
Cressing
Cressington and Grassendale
Crigglestone
Croft
Croft Spa
Cromford
Crook
Crossens
Cross Hands Halt
Crouch Hill
Crowcombe
Crowhurst
Croxley Green
Crumpsall
Cudworth
Culcheth
Culgaith
Culkerton Halt
Cullompton
Cutnall Green Halt

Daggons Road
Daimler Halt
Danby
Darby End Halt
Darfield
Darlaston
Darley Dale
Darlington North Road
Darsham
Dartmouth
Dauntsey

Davenport
Deepdene
Defford
Delabole
Denby Dale
Denstone
Dent
Denton
Derby Friargate
Derby Nottingham Road
Desborough and Rothwell
Desford
Devizes
Devonport King's Road
Dewsbury Central
Didsbury
Diggle
Dinting
Dinton
Disley
Doleham Halt
Donnington
Dorchester West
Dore and Totley
Dorking Town
Doublebois
Dove Holes
Downton
Draycott and Breaston
Drax
Drigg
Dronfield
Droylesden
Dudley
Duffield
Dulverton
Dunball Halt
Dunmere Halt
Dunsbear Halt
Dunsland Cross
Dunstable North
Dunstable Town
Dunster
Durston

Earlestown
Earswick
Easington
East Anstey
East Budleigh
East Langton
East Leake
Eastrington

Eccles
Eccleston Park
Eckington
Edale
Edenbridge
Edge Hill
Edington Burtle
Egloskerry
Egremont
Egton
Ellerby
Ellesmere
Ellesmere Port
Elmesthorpe for Barwell
Elmton and Creswell
Elswick
Embsay
Emerson Park Halt
Entwistle
Etherley
Ettingshall Road and Bilston
Evercreech Junction
Evercreech New
Evershot
Ewood Bridge and Edenfield
Exeter St. Thomas
Exminster
Exmouth
Exton

Fairfield for Droylsden
Fakenham East
Fawley (Herefords.)
Fazakerley
Featherstone
Felixstowe Beach
Fencehouses
Fenny Compton
Fenny Stratford
Fernhill Heath
Ferryhill
Filleigh
Finchley Road and Frognal
Finstock Halt
Firsby
Fishponds
Fiskerton
Fitzwilliam
Five Mile House
Fladbury

Flax Bourton
Fleetwood
Foleshill
Ford (Devon)
Fordingbridge
Forest Row
Formby
Four Crosses
Fourstones
Fowey
Foxfield
Frankton Halt
Frant
Fremington
Freshfield
Freshford
Fritwell and Somerton
Frizinghall
Frodsham
Fullerton
Furness Vale
Fyling Hall

Gainford
Gargrave
Garsdale
Garstang and Catterall
Garston
Garswood
Gateacre
Giggleswick
Gilsland
Glaisdale
Glastonbury and Street
Glemsford
Glossop Central
Glynde
Gnosall
Goathland
Godley Junction
Godstone
Golant Halt
Golcar
Gomshall and Shere
Gorleston Links Halt
Gorleston-on-Sea
Gorton and Openshaw
Gospel Oak
Goxhill
Grampound Road

Grange Court
Grange Road
Grateley
Great Ayton
Great Bridge North
Great Bridge South
Great Linford
Greatstone-on-Sea Halt
Greenfield
Greenhead
Green Road
Gresley
Gretton
Grimstone and Frampton
Grindleford
Grogley Halt
Groombridge
Grosmont
Guisborough
Guiseley
Gunnislake
Gwinear Road

Hadham
Haigh
Hailsham
Halberton Halt
Halesworth
Hall Road
Halton (Lancs.)
Halwill
Ham Green Halt
Hammerton
Hammerwich
Hampstead Heath
Ham Street and Orlestone
Handborough
Hanley
Haresfield
Harpenden East
Harringay Stadium
Hartfield
Hartley
Hatherleigh
Hathersage
Havenhouse
Havenstreet (Isle of Wight)
Haverhill
Hawkesbury Lane
Hawsker

Hayburn Wyke
Hayfield
Hayle
Hazel Grove
Heads Nook
Heathfield (Sussex)
Heaton Park
Heckmondwike
Hednesford
Hedon
Heeley
Heighington (Durham)
Hele and Bradninch
Hellifield
Hellingly
Helmshore
Helpston
Helsby
Hemingbrough
Hemsworth
Henbury
Hendford Halt
Henfield
Hensall
Henstridge
Henwick
Hesketh Bank
Hesketh Park
Hest Bank
Heswall Hills
Heyford Halt
Highbridge for Burnham-on-Sea
Higher Poynton
High Lane
Hightown
Hillside
Hindley South
Histon
Hole
Holme Hale
Holme Lacy
Holmsley
Holsworthy
Holt
Holt Junction
Honley
Hoole
Hope
Hopton-on-Sea
Horam

Horden
Horfield
Hornsea Bridge
Hornsea Town
Horsebridge
Horton-in-Ribblesdale
Horwich
Hucknall Byron
Humberstone Road
Hunwick
Hurstbourne
Hutton Gate
Huyton
Hyde Central
Hyde North
Hykeham
Hylton

Idmiston Halt
Ilfracombe
Ilkeston Junction and Cossall
Ilkeston North
Ilkley
Ince and Elton
Instow
Irthlingborough
Isfield
Itchen Abbas

Kegworth
Kempston Hardwick
Kenilworth
Kensal Rise
Kentish Town West
Keswick
Ketton and Collyweston
Keyingham
Kibworth
Kidlington
Kidsgrove Liverpool Road
Kildale
Kildwick and Crosshills
Kimberley East
Kingskerswell
Kingsley and Froghall
King's Cliffe
King's Nympton
King's Sutton
Kintbury
Kipling Cotes
Kirby Muxloe

Kirkandrews
Kirkbride
Kirkby
Kirkby-in-Ashfield East
Kirkby-in-Furness
Kirkby Stephen West
Kirkstall
Knaresborough
Knightwick
Knottingley

Lacock Halt
Lake Side (Windermere)
Lancaster Green Ayre
Langford and Ulting
Langley Mill and Eastwood
Langport West
Langwathby
Langwith
Latchley
Launceston
Launton
Lavington
Layton (Lancs.)
Lazonby and Kirkoswald
Lealholm
Leamington Spa Avenue
Leamington Spa Milverton
Leek
Leicester Central
Leigh (Lancs.)
Leigh (Staffs.)
Leigh Court
Leigh Halt (Kent)
Leiston
Lelant Halt
Levisham
Leyton Midland Road
Leytonstone High Road
Lichfield Trent Valley High Level
Lidlington
Lightcliffe
Lilbourne
Limpley Stoke Halt
Linby
Lincoln St. Marks
Linton
Littleham
Little Salkeld
Little Sutton
Littleton and Badsey

Liverpool Central
Liverpool Road Halt (Staffs.)
Liversedge
Llanymynech
Llynclys
Lockwood
Londesborough
Long Eaton
Longhope
Long Marston
Long Marton
Long Melford
Long Preston
Long Stanton
Longton Bridge
Longtown
Longwood
Looe
Lostock Junction
Lostwithiel
Loughborough Central
Louth
Lowdham
Lower Ince
Lowestoft North
Low Moor
Lowthorpe
Lowton St. Mary's
Lubenham
Luckett
Luffenham
Luton Bute Street
Luton Hoo for New Mill End
Lutterworth
Luxulyan
Lydd-on-Sea Halt
Lydd Town
Lydford
Lydney Town
Lyme Regis
Lympstone
Lyng Halt

Mablethorpe
Maddaford Moor Halt
Maiden Newton
Maldon East and Heybridge
Malvern Wells
Mangotsfield
Manningford Halt
Manningham

Mansfield Town
Mansfield Woodhouse
Manton
Marazion
Mardock
Marfleet
Marishes Road
Market Weighton
Marsden
Marsh Gibbon and Powndon
Marsh Lane and Strand Road
Marston Magna
Martock
Masbury Halt
Matlock Bath
Mayfield (Sussex)
Medstead and Four Marks
Meeth Halt
Meir
Melksham
Melmerby
Melton Constable
Melton Mowbray Town
Menheniot
Menston
Mersey Road and Aigburth
Mickleton
Middleton (Lancs.)
Middleton-in-Teesdale
Middleton Junction
Middlewood Lower
Midford
Midgham
Midsomer Norton South
Midville
Milborne Port Halt
Milcote Halt
Miles Platting
Millbrook (Beds.)
Miller's Dale for Tideswell
Mill Hill (Isle of Wight)
Mill Hill (Lancs.)
Millhouses and Ecclesall
Millom
Milnthorpe
Milverton (Somerset)
Minehead
Minety and Ashton Keynes
Mitcheldean Road
Moira
Montacute

Monton Green
Montpelier
Moor Row
Morchard Road
Morcott
Morebath Halt
Morebath Junction Halt
Morecambe Euston Road
Mortehoe and Woolacombe
Mossley (Lancs.)
Mottisfont
Moulton (Yorks.)
Mountfield Halt
Mow Cop and Scholar Green
Mumby Road
Mundesley-on-Sea

Nanstallon Halt
Nantwich
Narborough
Neston North
Nethertown
Newark Castle
New Basford
Newbiggin
New Biggin
New Bolingbroke
Newcastle (Staffs.)
Newchapel and Goldenhill
Newchurch Halt
New Holland Pier
New Holland Town
Newland Halt
Newlay
New Longton and Hutton
New Mills Newtown
Newnham
New Passage Halt
Newport Pagnell
Newport (Isle of Wight)
Newport (Salop)
New Romney
Newsham
Newstead
Newton
Newton Heath
Newton Kyme
Newton-le-Willows
Newton Poppleford
Newton St. Cyres
Normacot

Northampton Bridge Street
North Elmham
Northenden
North Filton Platform
Northorpe North Road
North Seaton
North Tawton
North Thoresby
North Wylam
Norton Bridge
Norton Halt
Nottingham Victoria
Nunthorpe
Nutfield

Oakamoor
Oakham
Oakington
Oakle Street
Oakley (Hants)
Oaksey Halt
Old Dalby
Old Hill High Street Halt
Oldland Common
Ormesby (Yorks.)
Orrell
Ossett
Otley
Otterham
Ottery St. Mary
Ottringham
Oulton Broad South
Oundle
Overton

Padbury
Padstow
Pallion
Pampisford
Pans Lane Halt
Pant (Salop)
Park (Manchester)
Parkhouse Halt
Park Leaze Halt
Park Street and Frogmore
Partington
Partridge Green
Paston and Knapton
Patney and Chirton
Patricroft
Patrington

117

Peak Forest for Peak Dale
Pear Tree and Normanton
Pebworth Halt
Pegswood
Pelsall
Pemberton
Penda's Way
Pendleton
Penns
Penruddock
Penshaw
Penshurst
Penwortham Cop Lane
Petrockstow
Pewsey
Pickering
Piercebridge
Pill
Pilning Low Level
Pinhoe
Pitts Hill
Pleasington
Plumpton (Sussex)
Pocklington
Point Pleasant
Polsloe Bridge Halt
Pontefract Monkhill
Pontefract Tanshelf
Pool-in-Wharfedale
Poppleton
Port Isaac Road
Portishead
Porton
Portsmouth Arms
Powerstock
Poyle, for Stanwell Moor, Halt
Poyle Estate Halt
Prees
Prescot
Preston Road (Lancs.)
Prestwich
Pudsey Greenside
Pudsey Lowtown
Purton
Puxton and Worle
Pye Bridge
Pylle Halt

Quintrel Downs

Radcliffe Central (Lancs.)
Radford

Radstock North
Radway Green and Barthomley
Rainford Junction
Rainhill
Ramsbottom
Ravenglass
Ravenscar
Rawcliffe
Rawtenstall
Reddish South
Redland
Repton and Willington
Ribblehead
Richmond (Yorks.)
Ridgmont
Riding Mill
Ringstead and Addington
Ringwood
Ripon
Roade
Robin Hood's Bay
Roby
Rocester
Roche
Rockingham
Rodmarton Platform
Rolleston Junction
Romaldkirk
Ropley
Rose Hill Marple
Rossett
Ross-on-Wye
Rotherfield and Mark Cross
Rowfant
Rowsley
Royston and Notton
Royton
Rudgwick
Rugby Central
Rugeley Town
Rushwick Halt
Ruswarp
Ryburgh
Ryde St. John's Road (Isle of Wight)
Rye
Rye Hill and Burstwick

Saddleworth
Saffron Walden
St. Albans Abbey
St. Andrew's Road

St. Bees
St. Budeaux Victoria Road
St. Columb Road
St. Helens Shaw Street
St. Ives (Cornwall)
St. Ives (Hunts.)
St. James Park Halt
St. Kew Highway
St. Keyne Halt
St. Michaels
St. Peters
Saltaire
Saltmarshe
Sampford Courtenay
Sampford Peverell Halt
Sandown (Isle of Wight)
Sandplace Halt
Savernake for Marlborough
Saxmundham
Scale Hall
Scholes
Scorrier
Scorton
Scotswood
Seaforth and Litherland
Sea Mills
Seascale
Seaton (Devon)
Seaton (Rutland)
Seaton Delaval
Seaton Junction
Seend
Seghill
Sellafield
Semington Halt
Semley
Settle
Severn Beach
Severn Bridge
Shalford
Shanklin (Isle of Wight)
Shap
Shapwick
Sharpness
Sheepbridge
Shepley
Shepton Mallet Charlton Road
Sherburn-in-Elmet
Shildon
Shillingstone
Shipton for Burford
Shirebrook West

Shirehampton
Shoscombe and Single Hill Halt
Shrivenham
Sidley
Sidmouth
Sidmouth Junction
Sigglesthorne
Sileby
Silecroft
Silloth
Silverdale (Staffs.)
Silverton
Skegness
Skelmanthorpe
Slaithwaite
Sleights
Slinfold
Snaith
Somersham
South Acton
Southam Road and Harbury
Southcoates
Southease and Rodmell Halt
South Elmsall
South Molton
Southrey
South Tottenham
Southwater
Sparkford
Speeton
Spofforth
Spondon
Spon Lane
Stacksteads
Staines West
Stainton Dale
Stalbridge
Stamford Bridge
Stamford Town
Standon
Stanley (Yorks.)
Stanley Bridge Halt
Stanlow and Thornton
Stanton Gate
Stapleford and Sandiacre
Staple Hill
Starbeck
Starcross for Exmouth
Staverton Halt
Steeton and Silsden
Stepney
Steventon

Stewartby
Steyning
Stickney
Stixwould
Stockbridge
Stockport Tiviot Dale
Stocksmoor
Stogumber
Stoke (Suffolk)
Stoke Edith
Stoke Works
Stonegate
Stonehouse Bristol Road
Stoulton
Stow Bedon
Stratton Park Halt
Streetly
Strines
Stubbins
Sturmer
Sturminster Newton
Suckley
Sudbury (Suffolk)
Summerseat
Sutton Junction
Sutton-on-Hull
Sutton-on-Sea
Sutton Park
Swanbourne
Swavesey
Swimbridge
Swinderby
Swine
Syston

Tackley Halt
Tadcaster
Tanhouse Lane
Tattenhall Road
Tavistock North
Tebay
Templecombe
Tetbury
Thatto Heath
Theddingworth
Thorner
Thorney and Kingsbury Halt
Thornford Bridge Halt
Thornton Abbey
Thornton-in-Craven
Thorp Arch
Thorpe (Northants.)
Thorpe Culvert

Thorpeness Halt
Thrapston Bridge Street
Three Oaks and Guestling Halt
Threlkeld
Thurgarton
Tinker's Green Halt
Tipton St. John's
Tisbury
Tiverton
Tiverton Junction
Todd Lane Junction
Toller
Tollerton
Topsham
Torrington
Tower Hill (Devon)
Trench Crossing
Trent
Trentham
Tresmeer
Trouble House Halt
Troutbeck
Trowell
Tumby Woodside
Tunbridge Wells West
Tunstall
Tyldesley

Uckfield
Uffington (Berks.)
Ulceby
Ulleskelf
Umberleigh
Upholland
Upper Holloway
Upton (Cheshire)
Usworth

Venn Cross
Ventnor (Isle of Wight)
Verney Junction
Verwood
Vulcan Halt

Wadborough
Wadebridge
Wadhurst
Wainfleet
Wakerley and Barrowden
Walker
Walsingham
Walthamstow
Wanstead Park
Wantage Road
Warmley

Washford
Washington
Watchet
Waterfoot for Newchurch
Watergate Halt
Waterloo (Lancs.)
Watford North
Watford West
Wath North
Watton (Norfolk)
Wednesbury Town
Welford and Kilworth
Wellingborough London Road
Wellington (Somerset)
Wellow
Wells-next-the-Sea
Welshampton
Wem
Wennington
West End Lane
West Grinstead
West Hallam
Westhouses and Blackwell
West Leigh and Bedford
West Mill
West Moors
Weston-under-Penyard Halt
West Pennard
West Timperley
Wetheral
Wetherby
Weybourne
Whaley Bridge
Whatstandwell
Wheathampstead
Whimple
Whitby Town
Whitchurch North (Hants.)
Whitedale
Whitefield
White Notley
Whitley Bridge
Whitstone and Bridgerule
Whitwell
Wickham Bishops
Wickham Market
Wickwar
Widford
Widnes Central
Wigan Central
Wighton Halt
Wigston Glen Parva

Wigston Magna
Willenhall Bilston Street
Willesden Junction High Level
Willington (Durham)
Willington Quay
Williton
Willoughby
Wilmington
Wilton South
Wimblington
Wimborne
Wincanton
Winchelsea Halt
Windmill End Halt
Wingfield
Winslow
Winston
Witham (Somerset)
Withernsea
Withyham
Wiveliscombe
Woburn Sands
Woodborough
Woodbridge
Woodford Halse
Woodgrange Park
Woodhall Junction
Woodlands Road
Woodlesford
Woodley
Wootton Bassett
Wootton Rivers Halt
Worsley
Wrafton
Wrenbury
Wressle
Wretham and Hockham
Wroxall (Isle of Wight)
Wylam
Wyre Halt
Wyrley and Cheslyn Hay

Yarde Halt
Yarmouth South Town
Yate
Yelvertoft and Stanford Park
Yeoford
Yeo Mill Halt
Yeovil Pen Mill
Yeovil Town
Yetminster
Yorton

PASSENGER SERVICE, LINE AND STATION CLOSURES

Passenger Stations and Halts to be Closed

SCOTLAND

Abbeyhill
Aberfeldy
Aberlour
Abington
Aboyne
Achanalt
Ach-na-Cloich
Achnasheen
Achnashellach
Achterneed
Addiewell
Advie
Allanfearn
Altnabreac
Alves
Alyth Junction
Anstruther
Appin
Ardrossan Montgomerie Pier
Ardrossan Town
Arnage
Attadale Halt
Auchengray
Auchindachy
Auchinleck
Auchnagatt

Back o'Loch Halt
Baillieston
Balado
Ballachulish
Ballachulish Ferry
Ballater
Ballifurth Farm Halt
Ballindalloch
Ballinluig
Balloch Pier
Balnaguard Halt
Balquhidder
Banavie
Banchory
Banff

Barassie
Barcaldine Halt
Barleith
Barrhead
Barrhill
Beasdale
Belses
Benderloch
Bishopbriggs
Blacksboat
Blackwood (Lanark)
Boat of Garten
Bogside Race Course
Bonar Bridge
Bonnybridge High
Borrobol Halt
Bowling
Breich
Bridgefoot Halt
Bridge of Allan
Bridge of Dun
Bridge of Earn
Bridge of Weir
Bridgeton Cross
Brodie
Broomhill (Inverness)
Brora
Brucklay
Buckie
Busby

Cairnbulg
Cairnie Junction
Calcots
Callander
Cambus O'May Halt
Canonbie
Carfin Halt
Carmyle
Carnwath
Carr Bridge
Carron
Castlecary

122

Castle Douglas
Castle Kennedy
Clarkston and Stamperland
Cleghorn
Cleland
Clydebank Riverside
Coalburn
Cobbinshaw
Comrie
Corkerhill
Cornhill
Coupar Angus
Cowlairs
Craigellachie
Crail
Crathes
Crawford
Creagan
Creetown
Crianlarich Lower
Crieff
Cromdale
Crook of Devon
Crookston
Crosshouse
Crossmichael
Crossmyloof
Croy
Cullen
Culloden Moor
Culrain
Culter
Cults
Cumberland Street
Cumbernauld
Cumnock

Dailly
Dailuaine Halt
Dalbeattie
Dalcross
Dalguise
Dalmarnock
Dalmellington
Dalmuir Riverside
Dalnaspidal
Dalvey Farm Halt
Dalwhinnie
Darvel
Dava

Daviot
Dee Street Halt
Dess
Dingwall
Dinnet
Dollar
Douglas West
Doune
Dreghorn
Drummuir
Drumpark
Drybridge
Dufftown
Duirinish
Dullatur
Duncraig Halt
Dundee West
Dunlop
Dunphail
Dunragit
Dunrobin Private Halt
Duror
Dyce

East Fortune
Easthaven
East Kilbride
East Linton
Eastriggs
Edinburgh Princes Street
Eglinton Street
Elderslie
Elie
Elliot Junction
Ellon
Elvanfoot
Eskbank and Dalkeith

Falkirk Camelon
Falls of Cruachan Halt
Fauldhouse North
Fearn
Findochty
Flemington
Forfar
Forsinard
Fountainhall Junction
Fraserburgh

Gailes
Galashiels

Galston
Garmouth
Gartly
Garve
Gatehead
Gatehouse of Fleet
Georgemas Junction
Giffnock
Gilbey's Cottages Halt
Gilnockie
Girvan
Glasgow Buchanan Street
Glasgow Cross
Glasgow St. Enoch
Glassel
Glenbarry
Glencarron Halt
Glen Douglas Halt
Glenfarg
Glenluce
Glenwhilly
Golf Club House Halt
Gollanfield
Golspie
Gorebridge
Grandtully
Grange (Banffshire)
Grantown-on-Spey East
Grantown-on-Spey West
Grantshouse
Greenhill
Greenock Princes Pier
Gretna Green
Guard Bridge

Hairmyres
Happendon
Harburn
Hartwood
Hassendean
Hawick
Hawkhead
Helmsdale
Heriot
Highlandman
Hollybush
Holytown
Houston and Crosslee
Hoy Halt

Imperial Cottages Halt
Inches
Insch
Inveresk
Invergordon
Invershin
Inverugie
Inverurie

Joppa

Keith Town
Kelvin Hall
Kennethmont
Kennishead
Kentallen
Kershope Foot
Kilbarchan
Kilbirnie
Kilbowie
Kilconquhar
Kildonan
Kilkerran
Killiecrankie
Killin
Killin Junction
Kilmacolm
Kilmaurs
Kinaldie
Kinbrace
Kincraig
Kingshouse Halt
Kingskettle
Kingsknowe
Kinloss
Kintore
Kirkconnel
Kirkcowan
Kirkcudbright
Kirkintilloch
Kirkton Bridge Halt
Kittybrewster
Knock
Knockando
Knockando House Halt
Kyle of Lochalsh

Ladysbridge
Lairg
Lamington

Langholm
Langloan
Largo
Larkhall Central
Laurencekirk
Law Junction
Lesmahagow
Lhanbryde
Loch Awe
Locheilside
Lochluichart
Lochskerrow
Lochwinnoch
Logierieve
Longmorn
Longside
Lonmay
Lossiemouth
Lugton
Luib
Lumphanan
Lundin Links

Manuel
Maryhill Central
Mauchline
Maud Junction
Mawcarse
Maybole
Melrose
Merchiston
Midcalder
Milliken Park
Milnathort
Mintlaw
Mormond Halt
Mosspark West
Moy
Muirkirk
Mulben
Murthly
Musselburgh
Muthill

Neilston Low
Nethy Bridge
Newcastleton
New Cumnock
New Galloway
New Luce
Newmachar

Newmilns
Newseat Halt
Newtongrange
Newton Stewart
Nitshill
North Connel Halt

Old Kilpatrick
Orbliston
Ordens Halt
Orton
Oyne

Paisley Canal
Paisley West
Park
Parkhead Stadium
Partick West
Parton
Patna
Penton
Perth Princes Street
Peterhead
Philorth Bridge Halt
Philorth Halt
Piershill
Pinmore
Pinwherry
Pitcaple
Pitmedden
Pittenweem
Pittenzie Halt
Plockton
Pollokshaws West
Ponfeigh
Portessie
Portgordon
Portknockie
Portsoy
Possil

Racks
Rathen
Reston
Rhu Halt
Riccarton Junction
Riddings Junction
Rogart Halt
Rothes
Rothiemay
Rumbling Bridge
Ruthwell

St. Boswells
St. Combs
St. Fort
St. Monance
Salzcraggie
Sandilands
Sanquhar
Scotscalder
Scotstoun East
Scotstoun West
Shandon
Shankend
Shields Road
Shotts
Slateford
Southwick
Spey Bay
Springfield
Springside
Steele Road
Stewarton
Stobs
Stonehouse
Stow
Stragheath Halt
Stranraer Harbour
Stranraer Town
Strathaven Central
Strathcarron
Strathyre
Strichen
Stromeferry
Struan
Symington

Tain
Tarff
Tauchers Halt
Thankerton
Thornhill
Thornliebank
Thorntonhall
Throsk
Thurso
Tillicoultry
Tillynaught
Tollcross
Tomatin
Torphins
Towiemore Halt
Tullibardine
Tynehead

Udny
Uplawmoor for Caldwell
Urquhart

Waterside
West Calder
West Ferry
Whifflet Upper
Whistlefield Halt
Whiteinch Riverside
Wick

Yoker Ferry

PASSENGER SERVICE, LINE AND STATION CLOSURES
Passenger Stations and Halts to be Closed
WALES

Aberaman
Aberdare Low Level
Abergele
Abermule
Aberthaw
Abertridwr
Acrefair
Alltddu Halt
Amlwch
Arddleen Halt
Arthog

Bagillt
Bala
Bala Junction
Beavers' Hill Halt
Berwyn Halt
Bettisfield
Bettws-y-Coed
Birchgrove Halt
Blaenau Ffestiniog
Blaengwynfi
Blaenrhondda
Bodorgan
Bontnewydd
Bonwm Halt
Bow Street
Briton Ferry
Bronwydd Arms
Bryngwyn
Brynkir
Bryn Teify
Buckley Junction

Caerau
Caergwrle Castle and Wells
Caernarvon
Caersws
Caldicot Halt
Caradog Falls Halt
Cardiff Clarence Road
Carno
Carreghofa Halt
Carrog
Cefn-y-bedd
Cemmes Road
Chwilog

Clarbeston Road
Clynderwen
Cockett
Commins Coch Halt
Connah's Quay
Conway
Conwil
Corwen
Coryton Halt (Glam.)
Cymmer Afan
Cynwyd

Deganwy
Derry Ormond
Dolgarrog
Dolgellau
Dolwyddelen
Drws-y-nant
Duffryn Rhondda Halt

Felindyffryn Halt
Fenn's Bank
Ferndale
Ferryside
Fishguard and Goodwick
Flint
Forden

Gaerwen
Garneddwen Halt
Gileston
Glan Conway
Glandyfi
Glan Llyn Halt
Glyndyfrdwy
Gowerton North
Groeslon

Hawarden
Hawarden Bridge
Heath Halt Low Level
Holywell Junction
Hope Village

Jordanston Halt

Kidwelly
Kilgetty

Lampeter
Lamphey

127

Landore
Llanbrynmair
Llandderfel
Llandow Halt
Llandow Wick Road Halt
Llandre
Llandrillo
Llanerchymedd
Llanfair
Llanfairfechan
Llanfechain
Llanfyllin
Llangefni
Llangollen
Llangower Halt
Llangwyllog
Llangybi (Caern.)
Llangybi (Card.)
Llangynwyd
Llanharan
Llanilar
Llanpumpsaint
Llanrhystyd Road
Llanrwst and Trefriw
Llansamlet North
Llansantffraid
Llantrisant
Llantwit Major
Llanuwchllyn
Llanwnda
Llanybyther
Llys Halt

Maerdy
Maesteg Castle Street
Maesycrugiau
Magor
Manorbier
Mathry Road
Matthewstown Halt
Menai Bridge
Montgomery
Mostyn
Mountain Ash Oxford Street

Nantyffyllon

Olmarch Halt

Pembrey and Burry Port
Penally
Pencader
Pencarreg Halt
Pencoed

Penmaenmawr
Penmaenpool
Penrhiwceiber Low Level
Penyffordd
Penygroes
Penyrheol
Peterston
Pontcynon Halt
Pontdolgoch
Pont Llanio
Pont-y-Pant
Pool Quay
Portskewett
Prestatyn
Pyle
Queensferry
Rhiwbina Halt
Rhoose
Rhosgoch
Rhosneigr
Roman Bridge
St. Athan
St. Clears
Sarnau
Saundersfoot
Sealand
Senghenydd
Shotton High Level
Shotton Low Level
Skewen
Strata Florida
Talacre
Talerddig
Tal-y-Cafn and Eglwysbach
Templeton
Tondu
Trawscoed
Tregaron
Trevor
Troedyrhiew Garth
Ty Croes
Tylorstown
Undy Halt
Valley
Welsh Hook Halt
Whitchurch (Glam.)
Wnion Halt
Wolf's Castle Halt
Ynys
Ynyshir
Ynyslas

PASSENGER SERVICE, LINE AND STATION CLOSURES

Passenger Services under Consideration for Withdrawal before the Formulation of the Report

*Lugton–Beith Town

*Hamilton Central–Motherwell–Holytown–Coatbridge Central–Glasgow Buchanan Street

Berwick-upon-Tweed–St. Boswells

*Edinburgh Waverley–Duddingston–Morningside Road–Edinburgh Waverley

Haltwhistle–Alston

Aylesbury Town–Sheffield Victoria (Local)

*Kimberley East–Pinxton South

*Leicester Belgrave Road–Skegness

Crewe–Wellington (Salop)

Cheadle (Staffs.)–Cresswell (Staffs.)

*Grantham–Lincoln Central

*Palace Gates–Stratford

Boston–Woodhall Junction

New Holland–Immingham Dock

*Uxbridge Vine Street–West Drayton and Yiewsley

*Taunton–Castle Cary

Yatton–Wells–Witham (Somerset)

*Taunton–Chard Junction

Tiverton Junction–Hemyock

Exeter St. Davids–Dulverton

Churston–Brixham

Brent–Kingsbridge

*Launceston–Plymouth

*Truro–Chacewater–Newquay (Cornwall)

*Helston–Gwinear Road

*Newbury–Didcot

---

* Withdrawal already implemented.

*Newport (Mon.)–Brecon/New Tredegar

Gloucester–Chalford

*Cardiff/Barry–Pontypridd

Pyle–Porthcawl

Pontypool Road–Aberdare High Level–Neath General–Swansea High Street

*Merthyr–Hirwaun

Dowlais Cae Harris–Nelson and Llancaiach

*Whitland–Cardigan

*Swansea High Street–Neath General–Treherbert

*Neath Riverside–Brecon

Swansea Victoria/Llanelly–Pontardulais–Llandovery–Craven Arms–
Shrewsbury

Carmarthen–Llandilo

*Princes Risborough–Banbury

Radley–Abingdon

*Princes Risborough–Oxford

*Wellington (Salop)–Much Wenlock

*Wrexham Central–Ellesmere

Redditch–Evesham–Ashchurch

*Coaley–Dursley

*Cheltenham–Kingham

*Kingham–Chipping Norton

Shrewsbury–Hartlebury

*Kidderminster–Tenbury Wells

*Stourbridge Junction–Wolverhampton Low Level

*Hereford–Brecon

*Moat Lane Junction–Brecon

Havant–Hayling Island

Woodside (Surrey)–Selsdon

Haywards Heath–Horsted Keynes

---

* Withdrawal already implemented.

PASSENGER SERVICE, LINE AND STATION CLOSURES

Passenger Stations and Halts already under Consideration for Closure before the Formulation of the Report

ENGLAND

Abingdon
Adderley
Admiralty Platform Halt
Alcester
*Alford Halt
Alston
Alveley Halt
*Andoversford
Ardingly
*Ardley Halt
Arkwright Street
Arley
Ashton-under-Hill
Audlem
Avonwick Halt
*Aynho Park Platform
Axbridge

Bampton (Devon)
Beckford
Belgrave and Birstall
Berrington (Salop)
*Bickleigh
*Bilston West
Bingham Road
Black Bank
*Bledlow
*Blowers Green
Bolham Halt
*Bourton-on-the-Water
Bowbridge Crossing Halt
Brampford Speke Halt
*Brettell Lane
Bridgnorth
*Brierley Hill
*Brill and Ludgershall Halt
Brimscombe Bridge Halt
Brixham
Broome
Broom Junction
Bucknell

Buildwas
Bulwell Common
Burn Halt (for Butterleigh)

Cadeleigh
Calvert
*Cam
Cashes Green Halt
*Caythorpe
*Chard Central
*Charlton Kings Halt
*Charlton Mackrell
Charwelton
Cheadle (Staffs)
Cheddar
*Cheltenham Leckhampton
Chesterfield Central
*Chipping Norton
*Churn
Claydon (Suffolk)
*Clearbrook Halt
*Cleobury Mortimer
*Coalbrookdale Halt
Coalport
Coanwood
Coldharbour Halt
Coldstream
*Compton
Congresbury
Coole Pilate Halt
Coombe Road
*Coryton Halt
Cound Halt
Cove Halt
*Cowley
Coxbank Halt
Cranmore
*Credenhill
Cressage
Crudgington
Culmstock Halt

---

* Closure already implemented.

*Daisy Bank and Bradley
Dogdyke
*Donyatt Halt
*Dorton Halt
*Doseley Halt
Downfield Crossing Halt
Draycott
*Dursley

Eardington Halt
*Eardisley
East Halton Halt
*Eastwood and Langley Mill
Ebley Crossing Halt
Ellerdine Halt
*Elson Halt

*Farley Halt
Featherstone Park
Finmere

Gara Bridge
*Goonbell Halt
*Goonhavern Halt
*Great Longstone for Ashford
*Green Bank Halt

*Haddenham (Bucks.)
Ham Mill Halt
Hampton Loade
*Hampstead Norris
*Harmston
Harston
Harvington
*Hatch
Hayling Island
*Hay-on-Wye
Heath
Helmdon for Sulgrave
*Helston
Hemyock
*Hermitage
Highley
Hinton
Hodnet
*Honington

Hopton Heath
*Horrabridge
*Horsehay and Dawley
*Horspath Halt
Horsted Keynes
Hucknall Central
*Humberstone

*Ilmer Halt
*Ilminster
*Ilton Halt
Immingham Dock
Iron Bridge and Broseley

Jackfield Halt
*Jacksdale

*Keinton Mandeville
*Ketley
*Ketley Town Halt
Killamarsh Central
Killingholme Halt
Kingsbridge
*Kinnersley
Kirkby Bentinck

Lambley
*Langport East
Langrick
Langston
*Lawley Bank
*Leicester Belgrave Road
*Liddaton Halt
*Lifton
*Lightmoor Halt
Linley Halt
*Littlemore
Loddiswell Halt
Lodge Hill
Longdon Halt
*Long Sutton and Pitney

Market Drayton
*Marsh Mills
*Mary Tavy and Blackdown Halt
*Melton Mowbray North

* Closure already implemented.

*Mitchell and Newlyn Halt
*Mithian Halt
*Moorhampton
*Morris Cowley
*Mount Hawke Halt
*Much Wenlock

*Nancegollan
*Navenby
*Neen Sollars
*New Dale Halt
*Newnham Bridge
*Newthorpe (Notts.)
*Noel Park and Wood Green
 Norham
 North Hayling
 Northwood Halt
*Notgrove

*Palace Gates
 Peplow
*Perranporth
*Perranporth Beach Halt
*Pinewood Halt
*Pinxton South
*Plym Bridge Platform
*Praze
*Princes End and Coseley
*Pye Hill and Somercotes

 Quainton Road
 Quorn and Woodhouse

 Renishaw Central
 Rothley
*Round Oak
 Rowton Halt
 Ruddington
 Rushcliffe Halt

*St. Agnes
 St. Mary's Crossing Halt
 Salford Priors
 Sandford and Banwell
*Sarsden Halt and Siding
 Selsdon
*Shaugh Bridge Platform

*Shepherds
 Shepton Mallet High Street
 Slaggyford
*Somerton (Somerset)
 Staveley Central
 Staveley Works
*Stow-on-the-Wold
 Studley and Astwood Bank

 Tattershall
*Tavistock South
*Tenbury Wells
 Tern Hill
*Thame
*Thornfalcon
 Thorverton
*Thurnby and Scraptoft
 Tibshelf Town
*Tiddington
*Tipton Five Ways
*Towersey Halt
*Trench Halt
*Trewerry and Trerice Halt
*Truthall Platform
 Tweedmouth

 Uffculme
 Up Exe Halt
*Upton and Blewbury
*Uxbridge Vine Street

*Waddington
 Wanstrow
 Wells
 West Exe Halt
*West Green
*Wheatley (Oxon)
 Whetstone (Leics.)
*Whitchurch Down Platform
 Whitehall Halt
*Whitney-on-Wye
 Winscombe
 Wollerton Halt
 Wookey
*Wyre Forest

*Yelverton

---

* Closure already implemented.

(87549)

I

PASSENGER SERVICE, LINE AND STATION CLOSURES

Passenger Stations and Halts already under Consideration for Closure before the Formulation of the Report

SCOTLAND

*Barrmill
*Beith Town
*Blackford Hill
*Bonnyrigg
*Craiglockhart
*Duddingston
*Gartcosh
*Gorgie East
 Kelso
 Maxton

*Morningside Road
*Mossend
*Newington
*Rosewell and Hawthornden
 Roxburgh Junction
 Rutherford Halt
*St. Rollox
*Stepps
*Whifflet Lower

PASSENGER SERVICE, LINE AND STATION CLOSURES

Passenger Stations and Halts already under Consideration for Closure before the Formulation of the Report

WALES

*Aberavon Sea Side
*Aberavon Town
*Aberbargoed
*Aberbran Halt
*Abercamlais Private Platform
 Aberdare High Level
 Aberdylais Halt
*Aberedw
 Abergwili
*Abernant
 Ammanford and Tirydail

*Bangor-on-Dee
*Bargoed Colliery Halt
*Bassaleg
 Bedlinog
*Bedwas
*Boncath
*Boughrood and Llyswen

*Brecon
 Builth Road High Level
*Builth Road Low Level
*Builth Wells
 Bynea Halt

*Cadoxton Terrace Halt
*Cardigan
*Cefn Coed Colliery Halt
*Cilfrew Halt
 Cilmery Halt
*Cloy Halt
 Clyne Halt
*Colbren Junction
*Cradoc
*Craig-y-nos (Penwyllt)
*Cray
*Creigiau
 Crumlin High Level

---

* Closure already implemented.

*Crymmych Arms
*Crynant
*Cwmavon (Glam.)
Cwmbach Halt
Cwm Bargoed Halt
*Cwmsyfiog
*Cwmsyfiog Colliery Halt
Cynghordy

*Darran and Deri
*Devynock and Sennybridge
*Dillwyn Platform
Dolau
*Doldowlod
*Dolwen Halt
*Dolygaer
Dowlais Cae Harris
*Dowlais Top
Drysllwyn
Dunvant

*Efail Isaf
*Elliot Pit Colliery Halt
*Ely Main Line (Glam.)
*Erwood

Ffairfach Halt
*Fleur-de-Lis Platform
*Fochriw

Garth
*Glan-yr-afon Halt
*Glasbury-on-Wye
*Glogue Halt
Glyn Neath
Golden Grove
Gorseinon
Gowerton South
*Groesfaen Colliery Platform
*Groesffordd Halt

Hafodyrynys Platform
Hengoed High Level
*Hightown Halt
Hirwaun
Hirwaun Pond Halt

Kilgerran Halt
Killay
Knighton
Knucklas Halt

Llanarthney Halt
Llanbister Road
Llandebie
Llandilo
Llandilo Bridge
*Llandinam
Llandovery
Llandrindod Wells
*Llanfalteg Halt
*Llanfaredd Halt
*Llanfyrnach
Llangadog
Llangammarch Wells
Llangennech Halt
*Llanglydwen
*Llangorse Lake Halt
Llangunllo
*Llanidloes
*Llanstephan Halt
Llanwrda
Llanwrtyd Wells
*Llwydcoed
*Login Halt

*Machen
*Maesycwmmer
*Marchwiel
*Marteg Halt
Melyncourt Halt
*Moat Lane Junction
Mountain Ash Cardiff Road
Mumbles Road

Nantgaredig
Neath Riverside
Nelson and Llancaiach
*Newbridge-on-Wye
*New Tredegar
Nottage Halt

*Ogilvie Colliery Platform
*Ogilvie Village Halt
*Onllwyn
*Overton-on-Dee

*Pant (Glam.)
*Pantydwr
*Pantyffordd Halt
Pantyffynnon

---

* Closure already implemented.

135

*Pantywaun Halt
*Pengam (Mon.)
*Penpoint Private Platform
Penrhiwceiber High Level
*Penscynor Halt
*Pentir Rhiw
Pentwynmawr Platform
Penybont
*Pickhill Halt
*Pontsticill Junction
Pontardulais
Pontllanfraith Low Level
*Pontrhydyfen
Pontwalby Halt
Pontypool Clarence Street
Porthcawl

Quaker's Yard High Level

Resolven
*Rhayader
Rhigos Halt
*Rhydowen Halt

*St. Fagans
*St. Harmons
*Sesswick Halt
*Seven Sisters
Swansea Bay
Swansea Victoria

Taff Merthyr Colliery Halt
*Talgarth
*Talybont-on-Usk
*Talyllyn Junction

*Three Cocks Junction
*Tonteg Halt
*Torpantau
Trecynon Halt
*Trefeinon Halt
Treharris
*Trethomas
Trelewis Halt
Trelewis Platform
*Tylwch Halt
*Wenvoe

---

* Closure already implemented.

APPENDIX 3

ROLLING STOCK REDUCTION

Table No. 1

ANNUAL POSITION : LOCOMOTIVES, MULTIPLE UNITS & HAULED STOCK

End of:	Steam locomotives			Diesel and electric locomotives					Multiple unit stock			Hauled stock	
	Shunting	Other	Total	Shunting diesel	Shunting electric	Other diesel	Other electric	Total	Diesel	Electric	Total	Passenger carrying	Non-passenger carrying
1953	3,097	15,492	18,589	252	2	8	63	325	..	4,565	4,565	37,197	15,529
1954	3,035	15,390	18,425	311	2	9	69	391	70	4,632	4,702	37,215	15,847
1955	2,894	15,066	17,960	447	2	9	69	527	179	4,675	4,854	36,861	15,687
1956	2,758	14,769	17,527	600	2	9	69	680	453	4,939	5,392	36,130	15,163
1957	2,609	14,350	16,959	775	2	28	69	874	1,349	5,004	6,353	35,474	14,994
1958	2,371	13,737	16,108	1,091	2	110	70	1,273	2,417	5,261	7,678	34,325	14,926
1959	2,050	12,407	14,457	1,373	2	427	83	1,885	3,244	5,843	9,087	31,450	14,271
1960	1,741	11,535	13,276	1,708	2	842	133	2,685	3,820	6,430	10,250	29,841	14,871
1961	1,422	10,269	11,691	1,894	2	1,285	156	3,337	3,998	6,890	10,888	26,961	14,551
1962	978	7,818	8,796	2,010	2	1,673	176	3,861	4,074	6,958	11,032	22,575	12,482

139

Whilst Table No. 1 shows the stock at the end of 1962, and progressive reduction will take place as services are withdrawn, it must be remembered that review of the utilisation of the rolling stock fleets is a continuing process. Already examination has pinpointed scope for the withdrawal of a further 1,200 passenger coaches; it is reasonable to expect that by the end of 1963 the figure will have risen to 2,500. A further review of the steam locomotive fleet, following one made towards the end of 1962, is in hand.

The composition of the wagon and container fleet over the past ten years, divided into the principal types, is shown in Table No. 2.

Table No. 2

ANNUAL POSITION: FREIGHT WAGONS AND CONTAINERS

End of:		Goods	Mineral	Steel carrying	Others	Total wagons	Containers
1953	.. ..	457,213	592,803	44,020	13,074	1,107,110	29,111
1954	.. ..	456,508	594,652	45,584	12,946	1,109,690	32,403
1955	.. ..	455,515	595,264	46,614	12,542	1,109,935	34,223
1956	.. ..	453,947	587,274	49,867	11,519	1,102,607	35,833
1957	.. ..	454,061	571,553	54,540	9,960	1,090,114	40,212
1958	.. ..	404,685	542,241	51,920	6,680	1,005,526	47,421
1959	.. ..	377,062	513,164	49,585	5,449	945,260	50,151
1960	.. ..	376,913	512,849	52,098	5,138	946,998	49,071
1961	.. ..	372,459	508,816	55,279	4,989	941,543	48,296
1962	.. ..	327,762	464,199	52,221	4,409	848,591	46,535

There were no marked changes in the composition of this fleet, other than the introduction of the 24½-ton mineral wagon and a number of special type wagons to meet particular requirements. In 1958–9, and again in 1962, however, the fleet was reduced by approximately 150,000 and 100,000 wagons respectively. It has already been decided to make another reduction of 100,000 wagons in 1963 and further withdrawals are contemplated.

It is not practicable at this stage to forecast with accuracy the eventual size of the rolling stock fleets, nor the rates of reduction, but some immediate targets, taking into account all known factors, and assuming adoption of the plan and its progressive development, follow:—

	Stock at end 1962	*Estimated stock*
Main line diesel and electric locomotives	1,849	3,750/4,250
Coaches	22,575	15,000
Multiple units	11,032	..
Wagons	848,591	500,000
Containers	46,536	36,000

Some of these estimates can be regarded as conservative. All of them will require to be revised from time to time. The number of coaches will be continuously reduced through increased use of multiple units and reduction in high peak services. The reduction in containers refers to the present types and takes no account of the building of new types which will be required for Liner Trains.

APPENDIX 4

THE LINER TRAIN

THE LINER TRAIN

The description 'Liner Train' is applied to a conception of transport based upon joint use of road and rail for door-to-door transport of containerised merchandise, with special purpose, through-running, scheduled trains providing the trunk haul. It is envisaged as the future method for handling those flows of traffic, which are composed of consignments too small in themselves to make trainloads, but which aggregate heavy regular flows sufficient to support one or more trains per day.

BROAD OUTLINE OF METHOD

The advantages of the Railway are in the disciplined, safe, rapid movement of large tonnages at low cost. These advantages have generally been outweighed, firstly by the slow discharge of wagons, and secondly by the delays and damage inherent in collecting wagons in marshalling yards. The idea underlying the Liner Train is to by-pass both these obstacles to speed and economy. The expensive chassis of the wagon will no longer be marshalled, or be detained while goods are handled. Terminal delays will affect only the body.

The Liner Train then is a train of chassis which will remain continuously coupled. It will cater for the longer distance traffics and will run to a strict time-table calling for high utilisation of the stock. It will carry containers and, when fully loaded, it will have a gross load of 680 tons and a payload of 360 tons. The speed will be a maximum of 75 and an average of 50 miles an hour.

By their combination of speed, reliability in all weathers, freedom from damage or pilferage, and convenience of service, Liner Trains will surpass anything known by rail or road.

POTENTIAL TRAFFIC

The Liner Train aims primarily to capture full load traffic not on rail, and to handle remuneratively traffics which are at present carried at a loss on rail.

The traffic studies show that about 16 m. tons a year of freight which is on road would be suitable for rail if the right conditions for conveyance could be created. The traffic is of the right physical nature and it moves in heavy and regular flows between a limited number of places and over sufficiently large distances. The conditions which must apply are speed, reliability, minimum handling and immunity from loss and damage, coupled with rates at a level acceptable to the customer and remunerative to the Railway.

The assessment of the potential tonnage is judged to be conservative. It includes only traffics which have been identified so far by examination of the individual flows of traffic in the 93 m. tons initially judged to be favourable to rail. A more thorough-going examination of 130 m. tons rejected as unsuitable for rail haul by traditional means may lead to some addition to the 16 m. tons identified so far.

To the tonnage which may be drawn on to rail can be added about 10 to 12 m. tons of existing wagonload rail traffic. Much of it originates at private sidings and is consigned to stations. Most of this is unremunerative at present, but will be handled more cheaply by Liner Train. In addition, there is a lesser proportion of the very uneconomical station-to-station traffic which has favourable characteristics for Liner Train movement.

There is also the probability that, arising out of the Post Office plan to concentrate the handling and distribution of postal parcels at a small number of centres, and the Railways' intention to proceed similarly with railway parcels and freight sundries, the potential of the Liner Train conception will be considerably increased. The tonnage might be in the region of 3 to 4 m.

There is a probability that there will be a growth of shipment of overseas freight in containers. Handling at the ports would be considerably facilitated thereby. With containers built to international standard, Liner Train services for ports should be especially attractive.

The type of freight traffic under consideration, being largely composed of the more sophisticated manufactured products, has been largely lost to rail or, where still carried in the traditional manner, is not remunerative. It is just this traffic which can be expected to grow at least as fast as the economy as a whole, but the Railway cannot hope to stay in the business, and compete satisfactorily on the scale envisaged, unless a radical change is made in method of conveyance. The answer is considered to be the Liner Train.

The overall potential for growth of Liner Train traffic over the next ten years with a growth rate of 3 per cent. per annum, is, therefore, of the following order:—

	Million tons
Potential traffic not at present on rail, at least	16
Existing full-load rail traffic	10/12
Parcels post, parcels, and freight sundries	3/4
Total potential at present	29/32
Increase over next ten years	10
Potential by 1973 (say)	39/42

In terms of distance carried the distribution is expected to be roughly:—

	Million tons per year
70–100 miles	7·0
101–150 miles	13·2
151–200 miles	9·5
201–300 miles	6·6
301 miles + ...	2·7
	39·0

comprising anything that passes by road at present provided it moves regularly and in substantial bulk over medium long distances.

THE SYSTEM OF SERVICES

The first services will be non-stop runs between selected places covering the very heaviest flows of traffic. As the scheme progresses routes with intermediate stops will be introduced. Map No. 11 shows the routes under consideration and

143

indicates what the final pattern of services might look like, but the actual pattern will be planned to ensure that the maximum ton mileage is moved with the minimum number of trains. The greater part of the mileage will be run on the more intensively operated main lines in the country serving the areas where population and industry are dense.

The Liner Train routes will interweave in a manner designed to connect between them most terminals by through services. A broad pattern of movement over the country as a whole by groups of routes is shown below:—

	Forward direction	Return direction	Total
	'000 tons		
London–Scotland	620	710	1,330
London–Midlands–South Lancashire	4,880	7,160	12,040
London–Southampton/Portsmouth	230	360	590
London–South Wales/Bristol–Plymouth	1,460	1,350	2,810
London–Yorkshire–Tyneside	1,350	2,260	3,610
South Wales/Bristol–Midlands–Yorkshire–Tyneside	2,140	3,760	5,900
South Wales/Bristol–South Lancashire–Scotland ..	1,480	1,780	3,260
Other			9,460
Total			39,000

EQUIPMENT

The project requires new types of equipment virtually throughout, except for locomotives.

As envisaged at present, the wagons will be bogie vehicles to ensure stability at high speeds, with a platform $42\frac{1}{2}$ ft. long at a height of 3 ft. 1 in. above the rail. They will be fitted with the pneumatic brake and be kept permanently coupled.

The length and height of the platform depend on the dimensions of the containers. The international standard 8 ft. × 8 ft. container is difficult to accommodate within British Railways' loading gauge, but by designing a wagon with an appropriate wheelbase and with a very low platform it is possible to obtain completely adequate route availability for Liner Trains.

The containers will be built to the newly recommended international standard section of 8 ft. × 8 ft. The following are the principal dimensions:—

Type	Length	Width	Height	Tonnage capacity	Cubic capacity
	ft.	ft.	ft.	tons	cu. ft.
(1) Covered ..	10	8	8	5	530
(2) Covered ..	20	8	8	10	1,090
(3) Open	20	8	*	10	*
(4) Covered ..	27†	8	8	16	1,490
(5) Open	27†	8	*	16	*

* According to purpose.
† 30 ft. when road regulations permit.

In many respects, apart from the overall dimensions and the provisions for securing and lifting them, these containers will be similar to experimental containers being developed on the London Midland Region.

Containers will have the greatest possible width of opening at sides and end. This will give maximum freedom for loading them by fork lift or pallet truck.

Where the nature and volume of traffic justifies it, suitable containers to carry any commodity now carried by general purpose or specialised road vehicles, will be provided. The use of privately-owned containers, built within British Railways specifications, will be encouraged.

The maximum length of container planned at present is 27 ft. because of present regulations for road vehicles. The wagon, however, is designed to permit an increase in container length to 30 ft. or more.

DEPOTS

The task at the depot is essentially the simple one of transferring, very quickly and cheaply, containers of standard sizes between road and rail. The layout can be equally simple and depots will consist of a siding (or two), sometimes a line to release the locomotive, one or more cranes spanning the siding, a roadway, a park for road vehicles and containers, and a small building for the staff.

The depots, of which it is expected there will ultimately be about 55, fall into three principal groups. Large ones handling over 2 m. tons a year, medium ones handling around 0·5 m. tons to 2 m. tons a year, and a few small ones handling under 0·5 m. tons a year. Since the operation of Liner Trains will be restricted to only a few main routes, it will be possible to serve them through a small number of depots so that the capital cost of depots will be low in relation to their throughput and the unit costs of handling containers through them will also be low.

The depots proposed are marked on Map No. 11.

TRANSFER SYSTEMS

The transfer system must deal satisfactorily with containers of varying lengths, shapes and weights; it must be consistent with the use of standard road vehicles since the service should appeal to road hauliers and C licence holders; it must transfer to ground as well as to vehicle; and it must be so cheap and flexible as to give reasonable costs even when not in continuous use.

Many systems, both traditional and newly devised, have been studied. As a result, it is likely that the preferred methods will be the use of straddle cranes and gantry cranes, lifting automatically by means of pincer arms engaging in the base of the containers. At places of maximum and still growing intake and output, there may also be scope for application of the fork-lift principle developed to meet the special circumstances of Liner Trains.

ROAD VEHICLES

Few road vehicles owned by British Railways are capable of carrying the new heavy containers. It is intended to co-operate with British Road Services, with C licence operators, and with road hauliers, so as to avoid an expensive duplication of road transport. As necessary, the Railway fleet will be adapted to the changing pattern which the Liner Train will initiate.

Costs

The costs per unit of the equipment are:—

Train	£
Locomotive:	
Diesel	110,000
Electric	82,000
Wagon	3,000
Container:	
10 ft.	700
20 ft.	1,000
27 ft.	1,200
Transfer, major depot—gantry with two cranes	80,000
Roadway and sidings parking (specimen)	70,000
Road vehicle and two trailers	5,000

These figures, and in particular gantry and container costs, are on the high side for production runs.

The investment to provide the first stage of two trains serving five depots will be of the order of £2·1 m.

The cost to equip the country as illustrated on Map No. 11 will be of the order of £100 m.

To determine operating costs, the following pattern of operation has been assumed:—

Average train speed	50 m.p.h.
Average duration of intermediate stop	20 minutes
Minimum turnround at terminal	2 hours
Maximum load:	
Gross	680 tons
Nett	360 tons
Container maxima of 16 tons:	
Days in service	255 per annum
Locomotive—miles	135,000 per annum
Chassis—miles	100,000 per annum
Container—journeys	150 per annum

The direct costs of rail movement per capacity ton on this basis and at present prices will be:—

Miles	10-ton container		16-ton container	
	s.	d.	s.	d.
100	7	3	6	6
200	9	3	8	3
300	11	0	10	3

After addition of collection and delivery costs, estimated direct costs per capacity ton are:—

| Miles | Direct rail costs per capacity ton | | Road costs per capacity ton | Margin in favour of rail | |
	10-ton container	16-ton container	16-ton container	10-ton	16-ton
	s. d.	s. d.	s. d.	s. d.	s. d.
100	20 3	15 9	19 0	—1 3	3 3
200	22 3	17 9	32 0	9 9	14 3
300	24 0	19 9	44 6	20 6	24 9

As will be seen, except for the 10-ton container moved 100 miles, Liner Train costs compare favourably with capacity ton costs for the largest road vehicles at present permitted.

Recognising that tonnage capacity cannot always be fully used and that some empty running may occur at times, both on road and rail, comparisons of 75 per cent. and 50 per cent. utilisations of rail capacity with 80 per cent. and 60 per cent. utilisations of road capacity, follow:—

75 per cent. Rail Utilisation v. 80 per cent. Road Utilisation

| Miles | Direct rail cost per ton | | Road cost 16-ton vehicle per ton | Margin in favour of rail per ton | |
	10-ton container	16-ton container		10-ton	16-ton
	s. d.	s. d.	s. d.	s. d.	s. d.
100	27 0	21 0	23 9	— 3 3	2 9
200	29 9	23 6	40 0	10 3	16 6
300	32 0	26 6	55 6	23 6	29 0

50 per cent. Rail Utilisation v. 60 per cent. Road Utilisation

Miles					
100	40 6	31 6	31 9	— 8 9	+ 3
200	44 6	35 6	53 6	9 0	18 0
300	48 0	39 6	74 0	26 0	34 6

Applying these figures to the expected build up of traffic, it is estimated that the following will be the financial results:—

Year	Tonnage m.	Receipts £m.	Direct costs £m.	Contributions to systems costs £m.
1965 ..	4	7	9	—2
1966 ..	12	21	21	..
1968 ..	30	51	42	+9
1973 ..	39	67	49	+18

Conclusions

Studies have been taken to a stage where it is apparent that the Liner Trains concept is one of great promise for the Railways, and a very broad estimate of the contribution which a system of such services might make to the finances of British Railways by 1970 is £12·5 m. over direct costs. By comparison, full load general merchandise traffic at present on rail fails to cover its direct costs by £31·8 m. a year.

Design studies have been taken to the point where decisions on equipment can be made very quickly. Market studies will have to be taken further before the full scope of the route system can be decided, but, in the meantime, attention is being concentrated on two of the most promising routes with a view to making the case for operating a one-train service over each of these by late 1964. Services which are receiving this special study are a double round trip per day between London and Liverpool, and a single round trip per day linking Sheffield with London and Birmingham.

148

(87655) Wt. P.10064 K60 4/63 Hw.

S.O. Code No. 88–832*

Published in 2013 by Collins

HarperCollins*Publishers*
77–85 Fulham Palace Road
London W6 8JB

www.harpercollins.co.uk

1 3 5 9 10 8 6 4 2

First published for British Railways Board
by Her Majesty's Stationery Office 1963.
This edition 2013

A catalogue record for this book is available
from the British Library.

ISBN: 978-0-00-751196-9

Printed and bound in Great Britain
by Clays Ltd, St Ives plc.

MIX
Paper from
responsible sources
FSC **FSC® C007454**
www.fsc.org

FSC™ is a non-profit international organisation established to promote
the responsible management of the world's forests. Products carrying the
FSC label are independently certified to assure consumers that they come
from forests that are managed to meet the social, economic and
ecological needs of present and future generations,
and other controlled sources.

Find out more about HarperCollins and the environment at
www.harpercollins.co.uk/green

BRITISH RAILWAYS BOARD

The Reshaping
of British Railways

PART 2: MAPS

The Reshaping of British Railways

REPORT AND MAPS

LONDON: HER MAJESTY'S STATIONERY OFFICE

ORIGINAL FACSIMILE

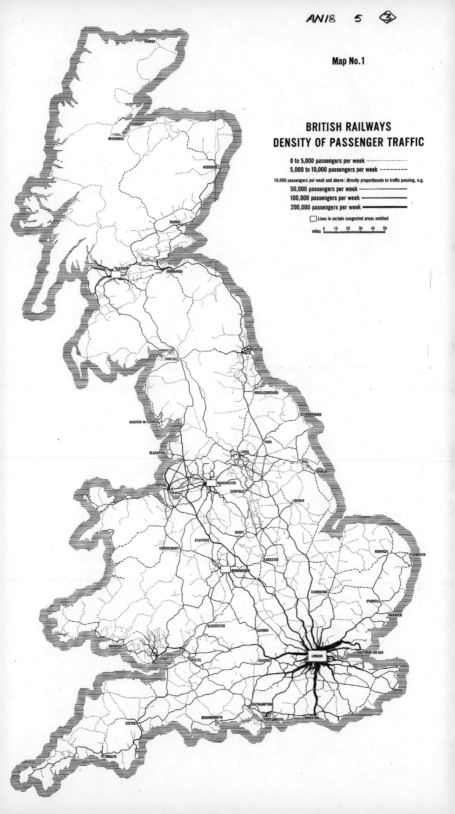

AN18 5 ③

Map No.1

BRITISH RAILWAYS
DENSITY OF PASSENGER TRAFFIC

0 to 5,000 passengers per week ·················
5,000 to 10,000 passengers per week ─ ─ ─ ─ ─
10,000 passengers per week and above: directly proportionate to traffic passing, e.g.
50,000 passengers per week ────────────
100,000 passengers per week ────────────
200,000 passengers per week ────────────

☐ Lines in certain congested areas omitted

miles 0   10   20   30   40   50

Map No.2

BRITISH RAILWAYS
DENSITY OF FREIGHT TRAFFIC

0 to 5,000 tons per week ··························

5,000 to 10,000 tons per week ----------

10,000 tons per week and above: directly proportionate to traffic passing, e.g.

50,000 tons per week ——————

100,000 tons per week ——————

200,000 tons per week ——————

▢ Lines in certain congested areas omitted

miles 0 10 20 30 40 50

THURSO

INVERNESS

ABERDEEN

DUNDEE

GLASGOW   EDINBURGH

CARLISLE

NEWCASTLE

MIDDLESBROUGH

SCARBOROUGH

BARROW-IN-FURNESS

BLACKPOOL

YORK

LEEDS

GRIMSBY

LIVERPOOL   MANCHESTER

SHEFFIELD

LINCOLN

SHREWSBURY   STAFFORD

DERBY

LEICESTER

NORWICH   YARMOUTH

BIRMINGHAM

CAMBRIDGE

IPSWICH

HARWICH

GLOUCESTER

OXFORD

SWANSEA

CARDIFF   BRISTOL

READING

LONDON   SOUTHEND-ON-SEA

DOVER

SOUTHAMPTON

EXETER

BOURNEMOUTH   PORTSMOUTH   BRIGHTON

PLYMOUTH

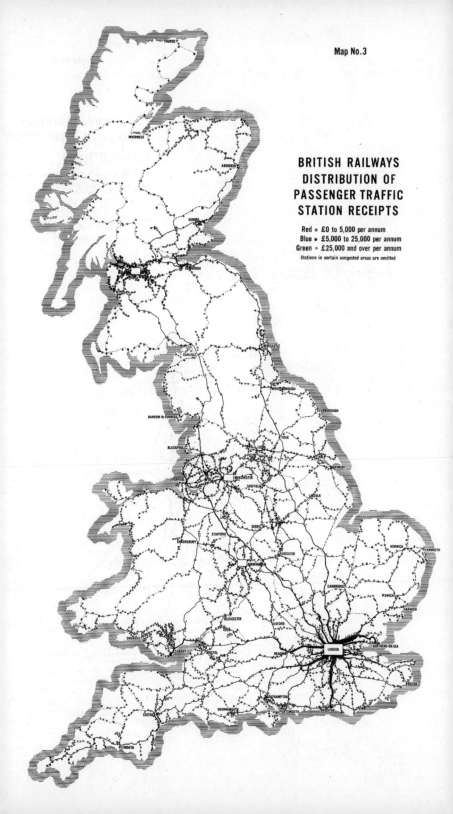

Map No.3

BRITISH RAILWAYS
DISTRIBUTION OF
PASSENGER TRAFFIC
STATION RECEIPTS

Red ● £0 to 5,000 per annum
Blue ● £5,000 to 25,000 per annum
Green ○ £25,000 and over per annum
Stations in certain congested areas are omitted

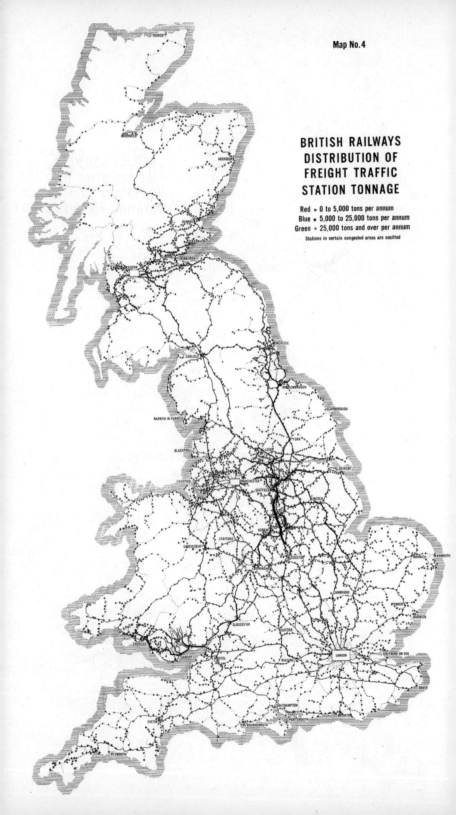

Map No.4

BRITISH RAILWAYS
DISTRIBUTION OF
FREIGHT TRAFFIC
STATION TONNAGE

Red ● 0 to 5,000 tons per annum
Blue ● 5,000 to 25,000 tons per annum
Green ● 25,000 tons and over per annum

Stations in certain congested areas are omitted

Map No. 5

BRITISH RAILWAYS DIAGRAM
SHOWING FLOWS OF FREIGHT TRAFFIC
(EXCLUDING COAL)
FAVOURABLE TO RAIL BUT NOT ON RAIL

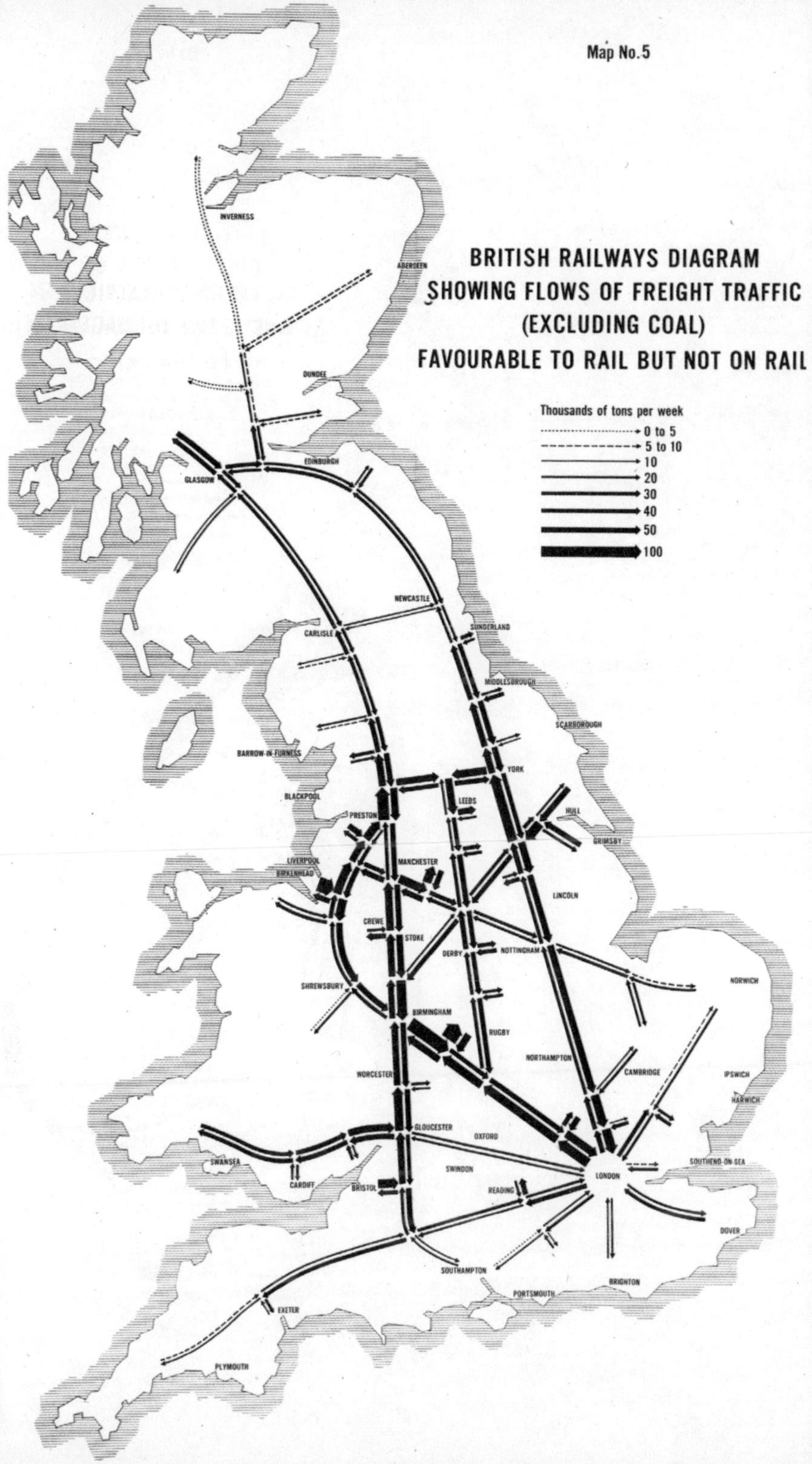

Thousands of tons per week

....	0 to 5
----------------------	5 to 10
────────────────	10
────────────────	20
────────────────	30
────────────────	40
────────────────	50
────────────────	100

INVERNESS
ABERDEEN
DUNDEE
GLASGOW
EDINBURGH
NEWCASTLE
CARLISLE
SUNDERLAND
MIDDLESBROUGH
SCARBOROUGH
BARROW-IN-FURNESS
BLACKPOOL
PRESTON
LEEDS
YORK
HULL
GRIMSBY
LIVERPOOL
BIRKENHEAD
MANCHESTER
LINCOLN
CREWE
STOKE
DERBY
NOTTINGHAM
SHREWSBURY
BIRMINGHAM
RUGBY
NORWICH
WORCESTER
NORTHAMPTON
CAMBRIDGE
IPSWICH
HARWICH
GLOUCESTER
OXFORD
SWANSEA
SWINDON
LONDON
SOUTHEND-ON-SEA
CARDIFF
BRISTOL
READING
DOVER
SOUTHAMPTON
PORTSMOUTH
BRIGHTON
EXETER
PLYMOUTH

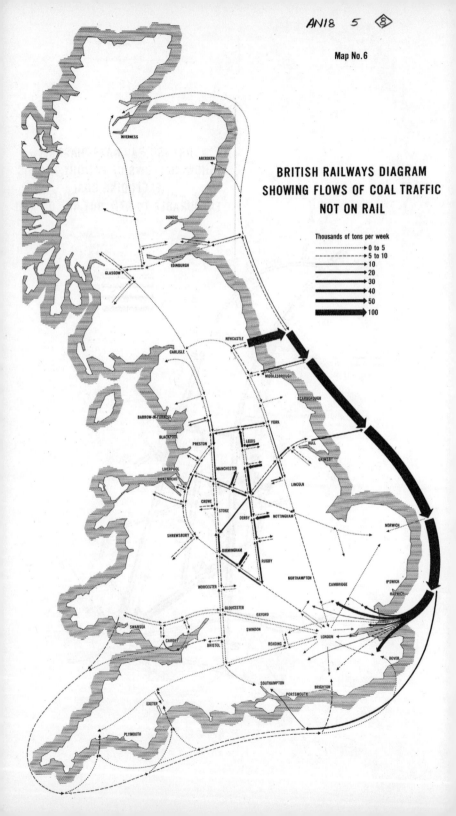

BRITISH RAILWAYS DIAGRAM
SHOWING FLOWS OF COAL TRAFFIC
NOT ON RAIL

Thousands of tons per week

⋯⋯⋯→	0 to 5
−−−→	5 to 10
⟶	10
⟶	20
⟶	30
⟶	40
⟶	50
⟹	100

INVERNESS

ABERDEEN

DUNDEE

EDINBURGH

GLASGOW

NEWCASTLE

CARLISLE

MIDDLESBROUGH

SCARBOROUGH

BARROW-IN-FURNESS

YORK

BLACKPOOL

PRESTON

LEEDS

HULL

GRIMSBY

LIVERPOOL

MANCHESTER

BIRKENHEAD

LINCOLN

CREWE

STOKE

DERBY

NOTTINGHAM

NORWICH

SHREWSBURY

BIRMINGHAM

RUGBY

NORTHAMPTON

CAMBRIDGE

IPSWICH

HARWICH

WORCESTER

GLOUCESTER

OXFORD

SWANSEA

SWINDON

CARDIFF

BRISTOL

READING

LONDON

DOVER

SOUTHAMPTON

BRIGHTON

PORTSMOUTH

EXETER

PLYMOUTH

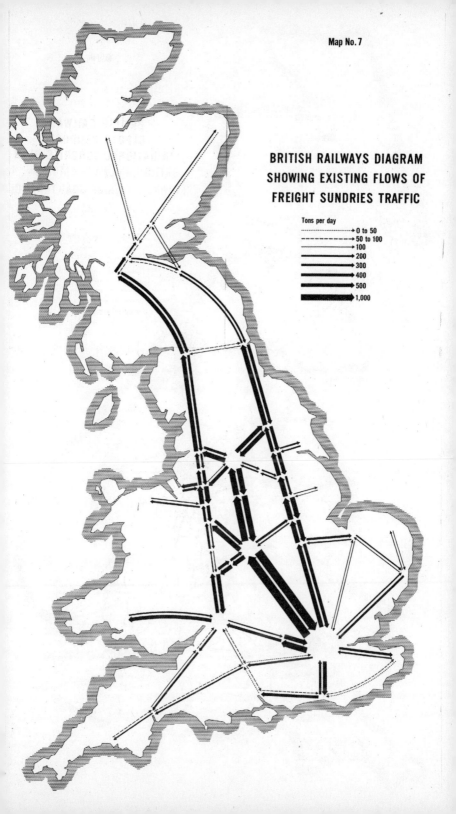

Map No. 7

BRITISH RAILWAYS DIAGRAM
SHOWING EXISTING FLOWS OF
FREIGHT SUNDRIES TRAFFIC

Tons per day

- - - - - - → 0 to 50
------- → 50 to 100
───── → 100
───── → 200
───── → 300
───── → 400
───── → 500
───── → 1,000

AN 18   5   10

Map No. 8

BRITISH RAILWAYS
DEPOTS PROPOSED
IN NATIONAL SUNDRIES PLAN

■ Main
▣ Residual Tranship

Map No.9

BRITISH RAILWAYS
PROPOSED WITHDRAWAL OF
PASSENGER TRAIN SERVICES

All passenger services
to be withdrawn ——————

All stopping passenger
services to be withdrawn ----------------

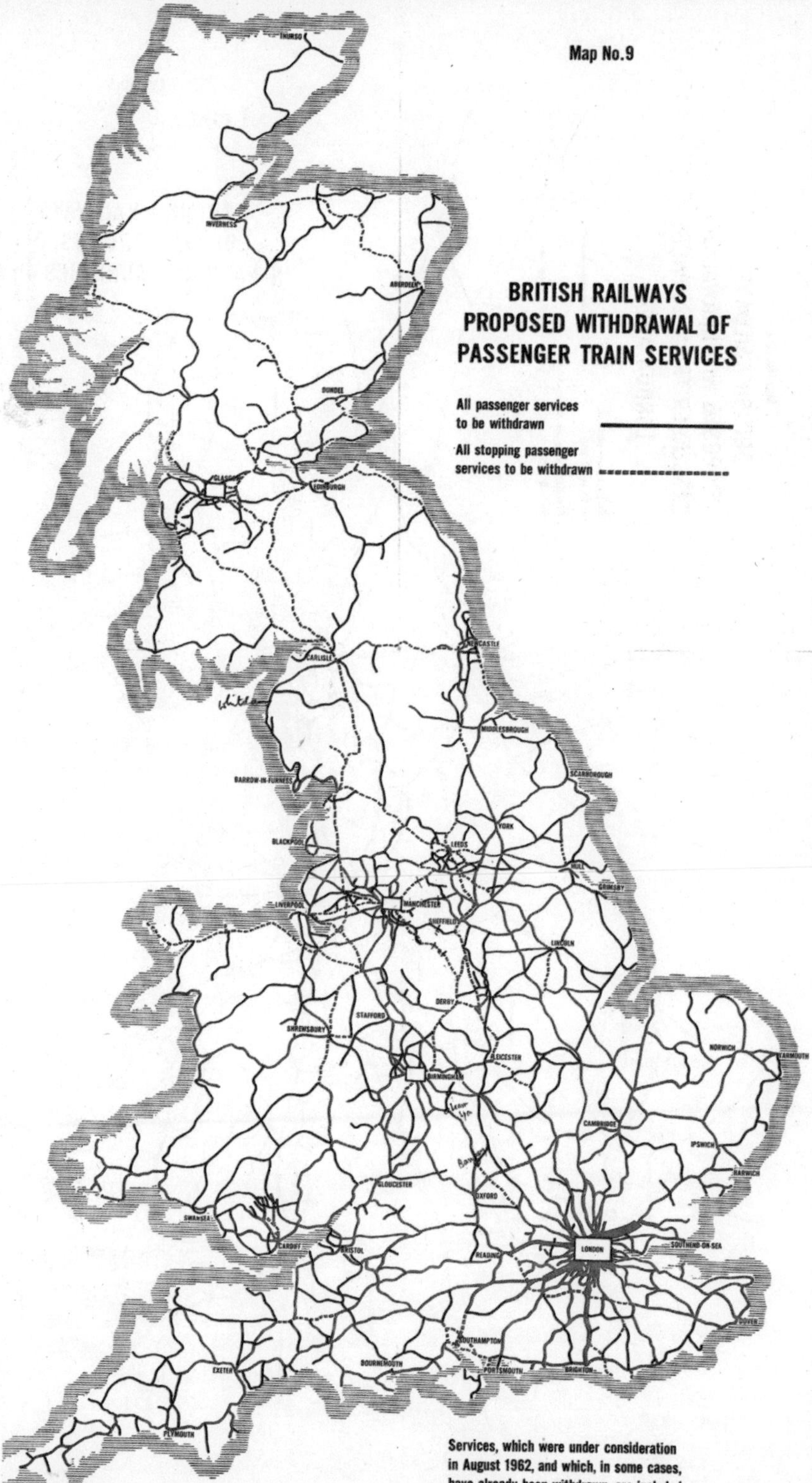

Services, which were under consideration
in August 1962, and which, in some cases,
have already been withdrawn, are included
in this map.

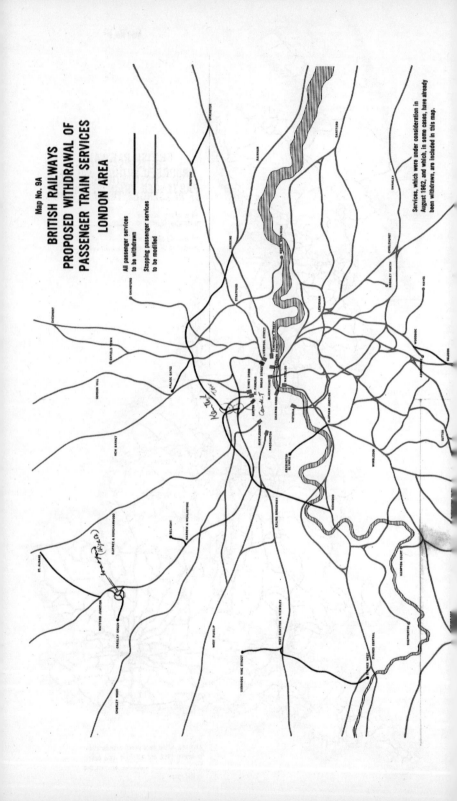

Map No. 9A

BRITISH RAILWAYS
PROPOSED WITHDRAWAL OF
PASSENGER TRAIN SERVICES
LONDON AREA

All passenger services
to be withdrawn

Stopping passenger services
to be modified

Services, which were under consideration in
August 1962, and which, in some cases, have already
been withdrawn, are included in this map.

Map No.10

BRITISH RAILWAYS
PROPOSED MODIFICATION
OF PASSENGER TRAIN SERVICES

Modification of services ─────────────

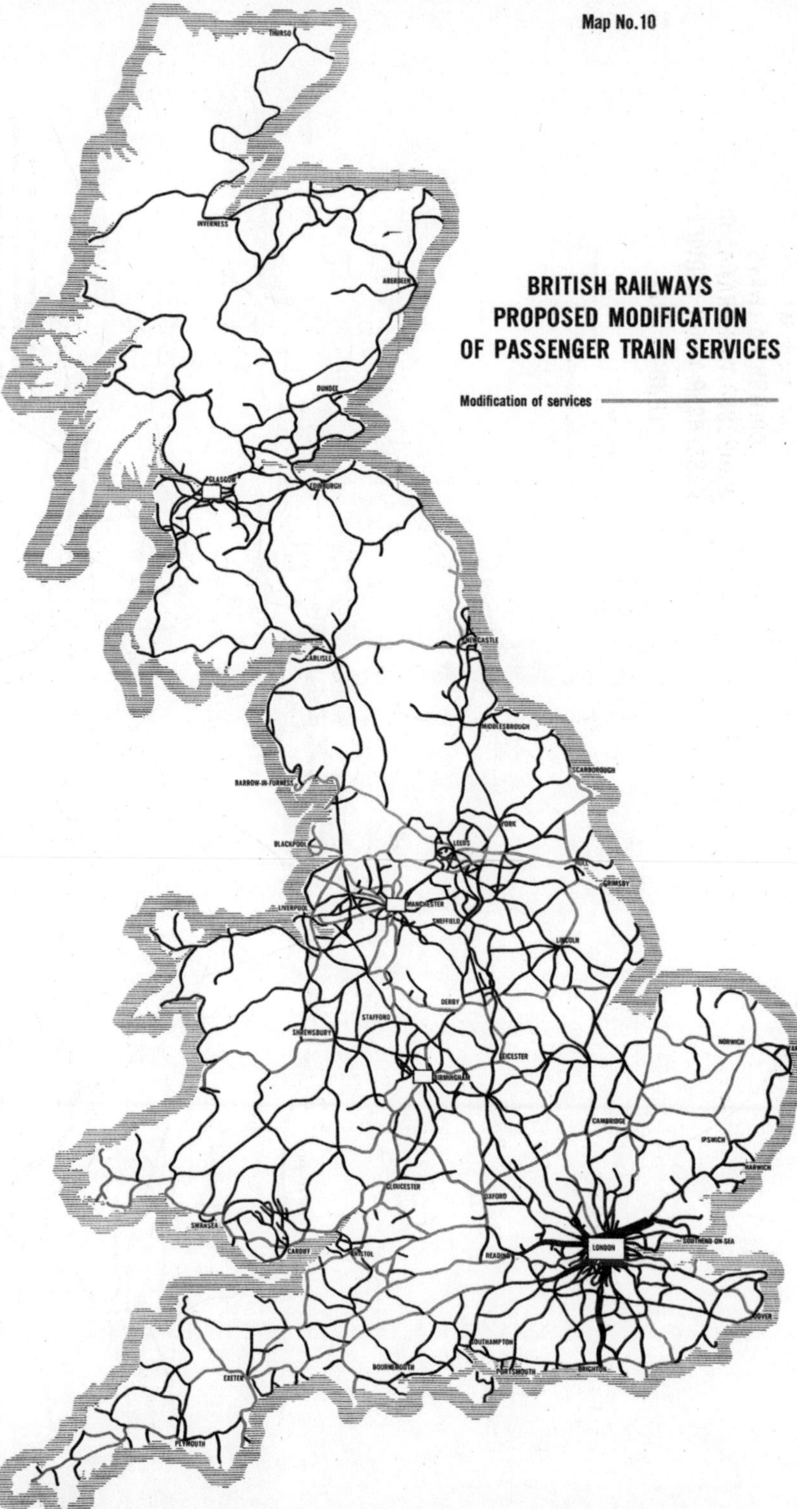

Map No. 11

BRITISH RAILWAYS
LINER TRAIN ROUTES AND TERMINALS
UNDER CONSIDERATION

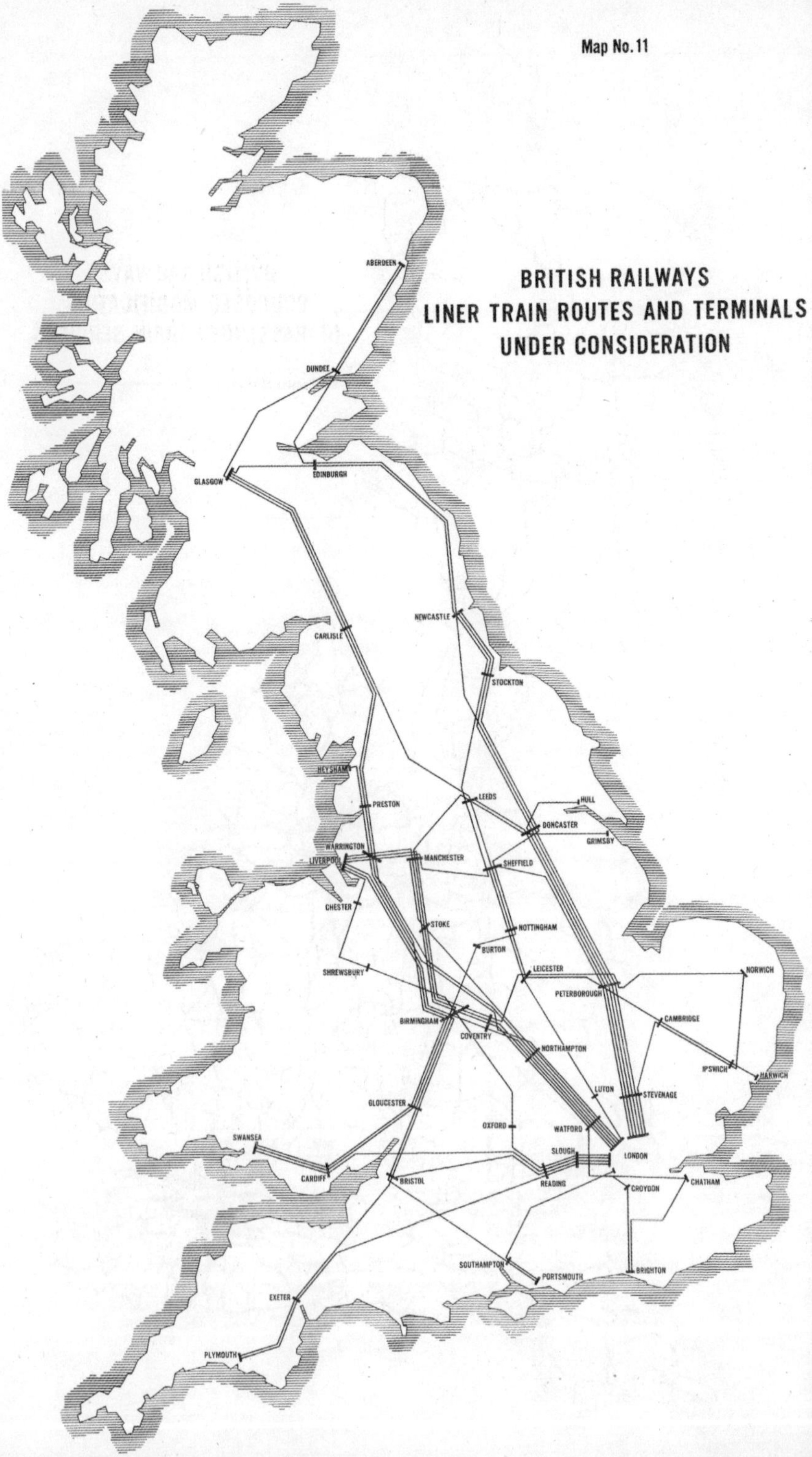

Map No. 12

BUS SERVICES IN BRITAIN
ROUTES COVERED BY STAGE AND
EXPRESS SERVICES

BRITISH RAILWAYS BOARD

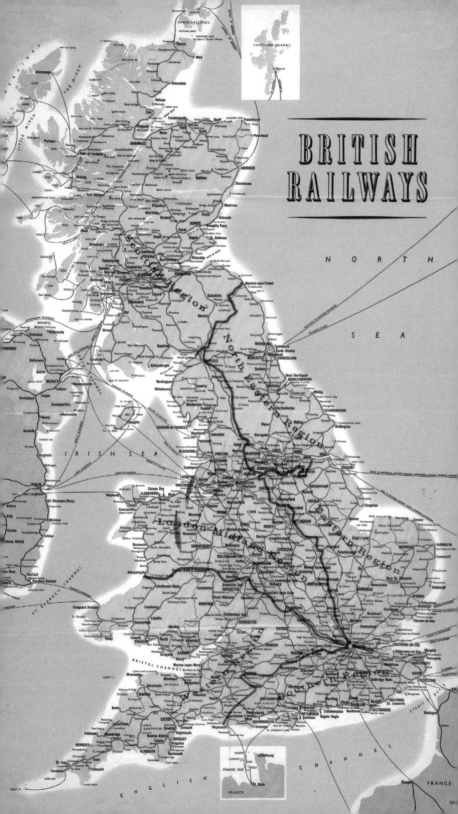